EAT
LIVE
SMART

Dr Anjali Hooda Sangwan, MD (Internal Medicine), is a fellow in Obesity Medicine & Nutrition Support from USA, where she worked for many years. She came back to India and joined Fortis C-Doc Hospital, Delhi. She is currently Medical Director at Center for Obesity and Longevity, running a very successful practice as a Functional Medicine & Advanced Metabolic Specialist. She is also a co-founder of www.livenutrifit.com, an app and web-based lifestyle modification programme.

Dr Anjali believes in a holistic, preventive and integrative approach while treating patients, especially for autoimmune and metabolic disorders (diabetes, PCOD, obesity etc.). She is a national level swimmer, a fitness enthusiast, a successful motivational speaker and a firm believer in 'Food is Medicine'. Spending time with her kids is her favourite thing to do.

Dr Anjali wants to create easy-to-follow health awareness through this book.

You can learn more at
www.doctoranjali.com
http://instagram.com/anjalihoodaMD
https://www.facebook.com/DoctorAnjali
https://www.facebook.com/LiveNutriFit
http://twitter.com/Anjalihooda

Anjali's book is an ultimate blend of functional and practical advice. Good health is a lifestyle, *na koi nuksan*, only *faida*. So there is no harm in reading and being aware of what one should not do.

—Salman Khan, Actor

An eye-opening book on the principles of preventive health, with powerful implications for our body and our life.

—Virender Sehwag, Cricketer

This book is about achieving a balance between physical activity, sleep, hydration, portion control, reading food labels and much more. Happy reading!

—Jacqueline Fernandez, Actor

This book holds the secrets to reversing obesity and India's Type 2 diabetes epidemic. Follow the plan and you will not only feel healthier but happier too.

—Dr Aseem Malhotra,
Cardiologist and International Bestselling Author

I would like to wish Anjali super success for her new book. It is a great read for anyone who is interested in nutrition and health and wants to have proper knowledge about how to take care of themselves. I think it is a Bible for every health enthusiast and a must read. I also wish the publishers all the best for this book and I look forward to reading many more of Anjali's books in the future.

—Sonu Sood, Actor

An invaluable guide to understanding nutrition, lifestyle and our bodies, and what each of us can do about it.

—Babita Kumari Phogat, Wrestler

THINK
EAT
LIVE
SMART

SECRETS TO SUPERCHARGE YOUR HEALTH

Dr Anjali Hooda Sangwan, MD

RUPA

Published by
Rupa Publications India Pvt. Ltd 2019
7/16, Ansari Road, Daryaganj
New Delhi 110002

Sales centres:
Allahabad Bengaluru Chennai
Hyderabad Jaipur Kathmandu
Kolkata Mumbai

ISBN: 978-93-5333-364-5

First impression 2019

10 9 8 7 6 5 4 3 2 1

Printed at Nutech Print Services, Faridabad

Contents

Introduction

I never call myself a diet doctor or a weight loss doctor. I am a healer and, incidentally, also a doctor who believes in changing lives through certain lifestyle adjustments.

Even as a doctor, I have had my own share of struggles with the weight gain and weight loss cycle. Eating too much too often, a sedentary lifestyle and the lack of a proper preventive approach had made me gain a lot of weight. When I had my first child, I couldn't even recognize myself—I had gained so much weight. I never went to any professional for help. Instead, I began starving myself and managed to lose some weight.

Such diets, however, never felt good. I was always tired, lazy and had severe mood swings. I couldn't walk properly; I had rashes due to my huge thighs rubbing against each other. I couldn't take care of myself and began resorting to food for comfort. I would go to a vending machine at the hospital and get a pack of peanut M&Ms, finish the entire pack and then feel miserable. I had no motivation to lose weight although I would think about it all the time. I started doing ten minute workouts at home since going to the gym was not an option, as I couldn't leave my kids after work. There were no workout apps at the time—even the iPhone was very new. I got myself a Denise Austin DVD and started a workout regime meant for beginners. I pushed myself very hard, but it led to major hunger pangs during the day. So, I decided to start working out at night.

A new problem cropped up—I was unable to sleep. After many hits and trials, I realized it wasn't the exercise but my food intake that was the problem. I started following the guidelines we used at my fellowship for other obese patients, replacing a part of my meal with proteins; I started reading labels on food packages. I found out that I was eating much more than I needed with regard to the concentrated calorie intake.

Now, this is a very important homework for anyone who is trying to lose weight. Assess your diet first and understand what is really wrong with it. I reduced my exercise and then started keeping a tab on what I ate every day. It became an interesting journey as I began learning about the food I ate and was shocked to know the truth about what we think is healthy. Bagel and cream cheese was my standard breakfast for a long time until I realized I should stop eating that every day and eventually, even the craving died.

Learning about macronutrients and how to balance them was the best thing that happened to me. I lost a good 2 kg a week and began feeling really good about myself. My productivity increased manifold and I became a much calmer person. Once I had tamed my diet, I started exercising much more, lifting about 10-15 kg weights easily and all with good nutritional support.

Although I was a sports person in my teens, I couldn't encourage myself to start a regime. I would join a gym, come back sore and would stop after only a few days. I was struggling, feeling edgy—so much so that even depression had set in. I was bringing up my children and struggling with their nutrition as well. I would never want anyone to go through the painful journey that I had to.

I had completed my Internal Medicine residency by then. I aspired to become a Nephrologist as I had lost my mother-in-law to a severe kidney disease. However, my weight was bothering me and I was lost about how to lose it. I was going through a medical journal when I stumbled upon a fellowship programme called, 'Obesity Medicine and Nutrition Support'—and suddenly, I knew what I wanted to do.

I remember my grandmother used to just feed me paranthas (fried Indian bread) and full fat yoghurt laden with sugar. I never really ate vegetables. It was when I went to boarding school that I learnt how to eat vegetables, as I did not have a choice. Even in school, I would eat more rice or roti (Indian bread) than dal (lentils) or vegetables. I don't really blame my grandma, as she didn't know much. She was also brought up on ghee (clarified butter) and roti and therefore, she fed us the same. I recall visiting my parents abroad. The drinking water was salty, so we would drink carbonated sweet beverages and canned juices instead. This practice was also equated with having more money. Looking back, these practices and habits had all contributed to my weight gain.

Let me now tell you a bit about this book. I like to think that I am one of the many women in this country who are working mothers and faced with the challenges of remaining fit, lack of time and feeding their kids good food on a daily basis in this era of junk food overpowering us. This is my opportunity to reach out to a larger audience. I would very much like to be able to help people by providing the necessary tools to help themselves as well as seek professional advice if and when necessary. It is commonly seen that people look for quick fixes, but weight loss is a game of patience and being smart about eating. Most people realize this only after damaging their system by experimenting with fad diets.

Everyone wants to look and feel healthy but most of us conflate this with being skinny. If you are thin, it doesn't necessarily mean that you are healthy. Weight loss has become a large industry and various kinds of solutions are available to us via the Internet, books and some quacks. It's important to have the right weight as per your height. Too much weight gain will contribute to health issues like diabetes, hypertension, Polycystic Ovarian Disease (PCOD), heart disease, stroke and even cancer.

Many books have already been written on this topic and I do not feel the need to write another weight loss book. Instead, this book should serve as a handbook for anyone who struggles to maintain good health. I will try to explain it simply without using medical jargon.

Here is how you can use this book to get the best possible results:

Prevention as a healthy way of life is not quite common in our country. Therefore, my purpose is to write a book that can serve people as a guide about when and how to seek help. In our country, most people approach doctors at a very late stage, when the illness has already struck.

This book is no magic wand; it's a practical guide meant to cover most aspects related to chronic non-communicable but preventable diseases in today's world.

Chapter 1

WEIGHT LOSS AND OBESITY: FACT AND FICTION

Let's begin with the story of a patient—a story that many will identify with.

> **Case study of a 26-year-old female who exercised excessively and had enormous guilt while eating**
>
> **Age:** 26
>
> **Sex:** Female
>
> **Weight:** 77.1 kg
>
> **BMI (Body Mass Index):** 27.8
>
> **Max weight till date:** 83.2 kg
>
> **Min weight in the last 5 years:** 72 kg
>
> **Previous medical issues:** Low Vitamin D, low HDL cholesterol
>
> **Exercise status:** Functional training/cardio daily (1-2 hours), Pilates three times a week, running daily in the morning (30-40 mins)

Diet recall: Non-vegetarian. Used to eating more proteins and less carbs and fats in the diet

Breakfast: Eggs

Lunch: Protein + vegetable

Dinner: Chicken/fish/protein shake/eggs

Snacks: Sometimes, and only green tea/coconut water/fruits

Social history: No alcohol or smoking

Sleep: 5-6 hours

Water intake: 4-5 litres/day

Supplements: Multivitamins and collagen

Medications: No medications

Plan: First things first, she needed to go easy on the workout as too much workout also leads to too much fatigue. She was provided with supplements like Omega 3 and Vitamins C, B12 and D.

She needed to eat balanced food composed of fats, carbs, protein and micros as well. She had been following a protein-rich diet for many years and had lost weight. However, her weight had now become stable and her body was no longer responding to a diet rich in protein. So a well-balanced meal was recommended to her to make sure that she was eating all the macros and micros. For breakfast, vegetable juices/smoothies were prescribed to her with eggs. Lunch was a usual meal with one chapati, vegetables, curd and salad. The snack options were coconut water, jeera, chaach (buttermilk) or nuts and seeds as she wanted something easy to carry to work. She was recommended protein shakes after workouts and finally, her dinner would be a combo of protein and vegetables.

There was some initial weight loss in the beginning but she did not enjoy her meals. She would have this constant feeling that by eating a diet rich in fat and carbs, she would gain weight—and that only proteins could help her lose weight. Because of this, she would sometimes skip her meals. If you see her diet recall, you will notice that she was following a diet rich in proteins with very little carbs and good fats. Her body became resistant to this diet and therefore, was not showing any results. So it became necessary to give her a balanced diet. This was the first step taken by us towards her weight loss journey.

When she came the next time, she informed us that she had not reduced her workouts and would also skip her meals. She focused more on the proteins as she felt that she would gain weight by eating carbs. She was depressed and anxious at the time, so it became very important to conduct some counselling for her. We explained to her how her habits were not helping her lose weight. She in turn explained that she did not feel energetic after her workouts and felt lethargic throughout the day.

We guided her gently and made her understand that too much workout was causing fatigue, and also that her diet needs to be balanced—including not just proteins but carbs as well to reduce this fatigue and stress. This time, we asked her to maintain a food log and send pictures of whatever she was eating so that we could make sure that she was eating what we prescribed. We also asked her to reduce workouts to just once a day—and that too, either yoga or the gym. We also included some supplements, like adaptogens, and herbal anti-anxiety medication to help her body relax. Curcumin was added to make her feel better.

She wanted to come more frequently so that we could monitor her progress. She started following her diet religiously, reduced her workout and was able to lose 1.7 kg within a week—and was feeling lighter as well. She was enjoying her meals and her diet was no longer restricted to proteins but also included a balance of carbs, fats and even the micros. She was maintaining the food logs and was sending us pictures of her meals daily so we could monitor her closely.

When she came to visit next, she was happy to have lost more weight, and some changes were incorporated in the same plan. The protein shake was removed as she needed to learn to eat real home-cooked food rather than depending on protein bars or shakes. The supplements were to be continued for some time.

Now, she is losing weight more easily by eating healthy and is no longer skipping her meals. She has been advised to keep maintaining food logs and to keep a diary of any symptoms that may arise with respect to the food she eats, so that we can monitor her progress. She has now learned to balance eating and exercising and to maintain regular workouts in order to stay fit. She is a continuing patient of ours and is happily losing weight and looking forward to more weight loss in the future.

Now, there might be a lot of health and weight related questions in your mind. Let me tackle each in a different section.

1. Do you need to lose weight?

Readers may wonder, why do I have to lose weight? Am I fat, unhealthy, or am I overthinking it because it's a fad? It is simple, really. Gaining weight might make you feel lethargic, clothes might not fit you anymore, you might feel bloated and you might feel like you don't like yourself anymore. You might even be told by loved ones to do something about your weight, sometimes you have a false target in your head to look like someone else, you have been diagnosed with a heart condition or you get diabetes or even cancer—all of these can be very compelling reasons to lose weight.

Why now?

If not now, then when? Many people go on with life without feeling the need to change, but when it comes to deeper medical issues, change is necessary. You could be a woman in your 20s or a man in your 50s but if you are overweight, it could be harming you physically and emotionally. Sometimes not liking yourself in the mirror could be the simple reason why you may want to lose weight.

Body Mass Index (BMI) tells you where you lie when it comes to being overweight or obese. BMI is a simple calculation based on a person's height and weight. The formula is BMI = kg/m^2 where kg is the person's weight in kilograms and m^2 is their height in square metres. However, it's only a ratio and doesn't account for high muscle mass; what really matters is the fat percentage. You may be thin but still have pocketed fat or even visceral fat, which is the fat around your organs.

You can calculate this through online BMI calculators and smartphone apps.

Waist circumference (WC), Dexa scan or skin fold measurements for accurate fat percentage are other ways to calculate if you are overweight. The day you figure out that you are overweight, you must start making small changes in your diet and lifestyle.

2. What makes you fat?

There are many factors that can make anyone gain weight:

    i.   Lack of sleep
    ii.   Lack of activity
    iii.   Not eating age-appropriately
    iv.   Drinking too much alcohol
    v.   Confusing boredom and thirst with hunger
    vi.   Eating too much
    vii.   Ageing and low metabolism with age
    viii.   Certain medications and undiagnosed illness
    ix.   Post pregnancy and childbirth
    x.   Eating disorders
    xi.   Genetics

You must sometimes wonder why some people never get fat. If you look closely at these people, you will realize that their lifestyle on the whole is much better than others. If you start noticing, you will see that they either eat slowly, or eat less, or are more active all the time. They don't plonk themselves on a chair all day, or they drink enough water throughout the day; they fast often, or are too young to start gaining weight. It's really a combination of things when it comes to remaining fit.

3. How fat is fat in the Indian context?

A lean body and a fat body can be differentiated not only by weight but—more accurately—by body fat percentage and waist-to-hip ratio. An apple-shaped body is more at risk of heart disease than a pear-shaped body. As we age, our body type tends to become more apple-like. Fat percentage is a good measure of assessing where you lie in terms of fitness. Fat percentage should be less than 30 in women and less than 25 in men approximately, as it also depends upon age, race etc. Dexa scan is the best measure of fat percentage, but many places offer handheld or scanning machines which will give you a rough idea of what your body composition is like.

Let me tell you about a patient suffering from childhood obesity. I had the pleasure of seeing this vibrant young 13-year-old boy whose mother had sent him to be treated for excessive weight gain. He opened my eyes to how today's teens are facing obesity-related issues and the reasons that parents are not able to do much about this.

This boy was in the 8th grade and had two or three tuitions daily. He was not involved in any sports as he had become lazy and overweight. He would feel most comfortable when he was at home on his bed. When I saw him, his only concerns were his tuitions and how he felt overburdened by that and school work.

I am not questioning anyone's parenting skills; however, I do feel that instilling the habit of good exercise at an early age is very important. A fit body will have an alert mind. I understand that there is lot of academic pressure, but if your child has poor health, he or she will not be able to perform at school to the best of their abilities.

The boy also shared how he was bored with the same food at home and therefore, loved to order food when his mother was not around.

I had an hour-long discussion with the child and the parents. I am no psychiatrist, but a large part of my obesity practice is counselling patients. Most people know that eating right and exercising is the right solution. But are we adequately provided with those solutions? It's easy to make a diet chart and send a patient home, but when they do go home, they start struggling again.

When I realized that this kid was fond of food, I immediately noted down his likes and dislikes and provided him with replacements for whatever food he loved.

Kids love pasta, noodles, chips, etc. These can be easily incorporated into their diets in a healthy way. A parent or a caretaker has to be counselled about the changes, and then it will be much easier to implement a healthier diet for their child.

Not appreciating kids and just burdening them with criticism and comparisons is not going to solve anything. Even unknowingly, parents often put that kind of pressure on kids. When you compare your child to his/her sibling or a peer, it can be very stressful for the child mentally. We, as parents, are the ones who should instill high self-esteem in our kids.

First, we should identify why our teenager is not listening to us. Hormonal changes in kids of that age are tremendous and therefore, valuing their efforts is of utmost importance.

So, coming back to our boy: as we progressed to his eating habits, he was surprised that I was allowing him to eat pasta, chips and pizza. Along with it, I also stressed the importance of having vegetables, fruits and salads. This boy went to school at 6 a.m. and had no time for breakfast. He would only have a glass of milk before leaving for school. How would his brain work? Also, the morning fat burning hormones were being wasted. His next meal would be at 11:30 a.m., which meant that the kid would be studying for five hours before he ate any energy releasing food. I felt so sad hearing this that my heart went out for this kid.

Some parents stop all junk food when they see a child gaining weight—especially if it continues after they come back from a visit to a pediatrician. The weight gain boggles their minds and all butter, cheese, fries and chips are taken away.

That is not the way you bring your child back to the path of healthy eating. You have to allow these young people to make healthy choices. Teaching them at school about nutrition is very important. If we load kids with sugar daily, they will have sugar cravings. Simple sugar is the biggest enemy of health, and it is present in almost everything we eat. There is no need for kids to have raw sugar such as table sugar, especially in milk or yoghurt—foods that already contain lactose. Eating sugar is a habit, and reducing that craving will be a slow process. Feeding kids fibrous vegetables, whole/complex carbohydrates and lean protein will take away their urge to have sugar, as the body's sugar needs will already be compensated. Sometimes, even desserts can be given, as it is impossible to tell your kid not to eat ice cream when there is so much visual stimulation for such food all around us.

So, my advice to parents is to seek proper help if your kid is facing such issues. Let a professional take care of them to start with and then, as they grow up, they will understand everything by themselves.

4. How do the gut and the mind affect weight loss?

The gut is called the second brain because it has the same serotonin receptors as the brain. We all know the old saying, 'We are what we eat.' Some foods make us happy and some don't do anything for us. There is an immense amount of bacteria and neuronal pathways in the gut. These neuronal pathways go from the mouth all the way to the anus. Thus, gut health is something that will influence your brain and body to behave in a certain way. Have you ever had a bad stomach after eating some junk food? You hear your stomach growling and wreaking havoc in your system. If you have a lot of gas in your stomach, it means that your stomach is on fire—or in other words, you have inflammation in your gut. Such gut inflammation can spread to the entire body over a period of time, if you continue eating the same unhealthy food. A healthy gut helps in your ability to deal with stress and enhances memory and clarity. That's why so many studies are being published about the role of the gut in depression and anxiety.

Case study of such a patient and how she got relief in just a couple of visits

Age: 35

Sex: F

Weight: 47.7 kg

BMI: 18.6

Max weight till date: 47 kg

Min weight in the last five years: 46 kg

Her main complaints were bloating, gas and reflux that had persisted for many years. Her endoscopy and colonoscopy results showed no abnormality.

Previous medical issues: Gastric reflux, migraine, bloating, acidity, uneasy stomach, constipation

Exercise status: No exercise

Diet recall: Non-vegetarian

Breakfast: Milk and bread

Lunch: Roti, sabzi (cooked vegetables), salad

Snacks: Cookies, namkeen (savoury snacks) or fruits

Dinner: Chicken, roti, sabzi

Plan: The first thing that she needed to do was change her diet. She needed to stop having too many fruits or dairy products and also needed to cut back on refined flour. Where there is an overgrowth of fungus, food begins to ferment rather than being broken down to get digested. The fermentation produces excess gas that travels through the intestine, stomach and into the esophagus. The other cause is underproduction of acid by the stomach.

I started her off with virgin coconut oil, probiotics (good bacteria that help in gut immunity and digestion) and apple cider vinegar, keeping gut dysbiosis (imbalance of intestinal microbes) in mind. Coconut oil acts as an antioxidant and prevents intestinal permeability by remodelling the gut microbiome (good bacteria), and apple cider acts as a probiotic.

If you see her diet recall, you can see the exact cause of her reflux—milk, gluten and fruits. Her diet was lacking in protein and healthy fats. She was having roti, sabzi and salad for lunch but I gave her an alternative to rotis—quinoa or amaranth, assuming a gluten sensitivity which may or may not have been there. I also changed her breakfast from milk and bread to eggs, except on Tuesdays. Eating 20-30 gm protein (depending on the body) for breakfast keeps one satisfied for a longer period as protein takes a longer time to get digested.

I advised her to have coconut water or herbal tea for any hunger pangs, along with frozen berries or fresh coconut. For the evening snack, I prescribed nuts like almonds/ pine nuts/walnuts and seeds like pumpkin/ flax, as they are a source of healthy fat. Protein and vegetables were prescribed for dinner as both reduce reflux symptoms.

It was a well-balanced plan, along with some eliminations. She came back after twenty-one days and she was happy to report that she no longer had any bloating. The constipation had improved and the reflux, too, had gotten better.

I asked her to introduce fruits, one at a time, to her diet and stay away from gluten and dairy products. I gave her the option of almond milk, which is a lactose-free milk. Almond milk is alkaline and therefore, balances the acid in the stomach.

Since the intestinal bacteria are altered due to toxins in food and the environment, the immunity of the body is weakened and it leads to various diseases like skin allergies and autoimmune conditions like rheumatoid arthritis, ankylosing spondylitis, hypothyroidism etc.

Case study of a young teenager with skin allergies

Age: 15 years

Sex: M

Weight: 100 kg

BMI: 34.6 (95th percentile)

Max weight till date: 100 kg

Min weight in the last five years: 68 kg

Previous medical issues: Atopic dermatitis on arm, neck and face, obesity, asthma during childhood, weak immune system

Exercise status: Gym, five days a week

Diet recall: Non-vegetarian but eats lots of carbs

Breakfast: Milk and muesli or (sometimes) eggs

Lunch: Chapati or brown rice with dal

Evening snacks: Fruits

Dinner: Chicken, chapati or rice

Social history: No alcohol or smoking

Sleep: 7 hours

Water intake: 3-4 litres/day

Supplements: None

Medications: Not on any medications

Plan: Atopic dermatitis, also known as eczema, is an inflammatory condition of the skin which can cause itchiness. First things first, he needed to stop taking sugar, as he was also having sugar cravings. As sugar helps the growth of opportunistic bacteria in our body, it can worsen skin allergy. Eating sugar is in any case bad and can create many health problems in people. I started him on a probiotic twice a day: one teaspoon of coconut oil along with curcumin to inhibit harmful bacteria and to boost his immunity.

He also needed to cut back on milk, bread, maida (refined flour), eggs, peanuts, walnuts, sunflower seeds, cashews, fruits, olives, mushrooms, tomatoes, brinjals, raisins, mustard, vinegar, sweets, biscuits and namkeen.

His initial weight loss started very easily when he gave up the forbidden foods and followed the prescribed diet plan I charted out for him. Since he had atopic dermatitis, he had to cut back on certain foods even though a calorie deficit was created.

If you see his diet recall, you can see the exact cause of his weight gain and atopic dermatitis. He had a lot of carbs, fruits twice a day, as well as milk. That's poor eating habit. He was a non-vegetarian but was eating even more carbs in the form of rice, muesli and chapati.

I first replaced certain carbs with a healthy form of food. However, he was a growing child and it was difficult for him to quit sugar and follow the prescribed plan at the time. Therefore, the first thing I did was to replace certain things that he was having with the healthy options. He was having milk and muesli for breakfast, so I replaced wheat muesli with amaranth muesli and instead of milk, I gave him almond milk. I substituted rice with quinoa rice or brown rice, wheat chapati with alternate flour (besan/quinoa/bajra/jowar/ragi) chapati. But he also had to start with nutritive food, so I gave him chicken keema (minced chicken) roll along with gluten-free products like quinoa. I increased his protein intake, as weight loss was also a consideration—dinner was only protein and vegetables. As he was a school-going child, the task was to give him lunch options for school too. I replaced his original choice, fruits, with oats pancakes, oats upma and moong dal pancakes. As he was working out as well, I prescribed him some heavy evening snacks like sweet potatoes and occasionally some nuts or oats poha.

He was an obedient child and followed the plan properly without cheating even a little. His sugar cravings dropped and he became more focused on his weight. For the allergy, he saw a change in himself and in three weeks, his skin allergy not only stopped increasing but, eventually, stopped flaring.

Since it was a well-balanced plan, I could easily see him at longer intervals. When he came back at the end of one-and-a-half months, he had lost 7 kg without ever feeling like he was on a diet. This time, I cut back his grains, although this made it tougher for him, and focused more on protein and vegetables. I asked him to follow this plan for three weeks as well, and his skin allergy improved with this plan. His current weight, after six months, is 75 kg. He has lost about 25 kg. His atopic dermatitis is better. I asked him to extend the grains-off plan for three more weeks and to continue with fish oil, curcumin and coconut oil for a longer time. He is now on a maintenance plan with some form of grains.

5. How do hormones affect longevity and obesity?

Optimizing your hormones is very important for losing weight. Therefore, it is advisable to learn which foods are working together for maximum endocrine benefit. Hormones affect metabolic rate and one's ability to lose or gain weight. After the age of 20, the metabolic rate drops about 2 per cent; after 40, it slows down 5 per cent per decade. There are many hormones that influence weight loss. Here are a few hormones which I shall briefly talk about for a better understanding of your health.

i. Insulin

The function of insulin in our body is to lower blood glucose. When we eat food, the food is broken down into simple sugars. Insulin takes the sugar and puts it into the liver where it is converted to glycogen for muscle use. Insulin is a fat storing hormone; it converts the glucose into fatty acids that are then used as fuel by the body. What triggers insulin release is glucose. Therefore, any food that has low glucose is expected not to raise the insulin level. Thus, the category 'low glycemic index'. Foods on the low glycemic index are—most vegetables, salads, most fruits, except when they are very ripe and sweet, most nuts, sweet potato, lentils, all sea foods, all meats, eggs etc. The high glycemic index foods are white flour pasta, doughnuts, pastries, candies and chocolates as they all result in high insulin levels, thus storing fat even further.

Insulin resistance is fairly common in our younger generation. However, it can lead to diabetes at a later stage if not addressed early enough. Crash diets, followed by bingeing, harm the pancreas and a body can thus become insulin resistant. Insulin resistance is also a pre-diabetic condition. This is most often seen in women suffering from Polycystic Ovarian Disease.

What causes insulin resistance?

The main causes of insulin resistance are a sedentary lifestyle, artificial chemicals in food, plastic use, skipping breakfast, stress, excessive calorie intake, excessive sugar intake, obesity, steroid use and medications. Insulin resistance is a prediabetic symptom.

Signs of having insulin resistance are:

Fat accumulated mainly around your waist
Acne
Depression
Hirsutism or facial hair in women
Insomnia
Irregular periods
Low libido
Infertility
Dark pigmentation around the neck and under arms

You may also have higher blood glucose/higher insulin during fasting or post meals, fatigue and altered liver function tests.

After you have recognized any of these signs, it would be a good idea to go and consult a physician.

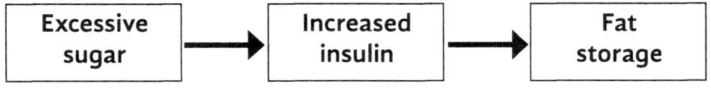

Case study of a man with undiagnosed diabetes

A friend referred his brother to me, primarily for weight loss. He was a man with a big frame, very pleasant and desperate for help. He had bad dietary habits and drank alcohol at least four times a week. Upon examination of his vitals, blood reports and the patient himself, he seemed to have a typical metabolic syndrome: obese, borderline high blood pressure, history of high cholesterol and high blood sugar. This was a red flag.

Going through his eating habits and current lifestyle, here is what I found:

Age: 33

Sex: M

Weight: 128.6 kg

BMI: 42.4

Max weight till date: Current weight of 128.6 kg

Min weight in the last five years: 96 kg

Previous medical issues: None

Exercise status: None

Diet recall: Non-vegetarian, diet consisted of mostly, eggs, fish, rice, bread and very few vegetables and fruits

Social history: Alcohol and smoking

Sleep: 7 hours

Water intake: Not a big fan of drinking water

Supplements: None

Medications: None

Plan: He needed a series of blood tests. He hadn't had a physical check-up done in over a year.

The second most important thing was that he needed immense counselling on avoiding alcohol and cigarettes. He understood and was very happy to comply, in just one visit. It was very impressive, as it usually takes a few visits before patients actually understand and put this to action.

The third aspect was the initiation of medication and supplements. He was given fish oil as a prime supplement, with others.

His diet was not balanced and he would end up eating junk, especially in the evenings. His wife was with him when he first came to see me and she was a very supportive woman. She was more concerned about him than he was. They were going to be parents soon.

So, diet counselling and a tentative plan was given. He was given regular food, balanced with carbs, proteins and fats, with vegetables, healthy snacks, nuts, seeds etc.

He would sometimes skip lunch. But from then on, he was going to pack lunch from home. His wife would ensure that under my supervision.

When the reports came back, my suspicion of diabetes proved to be right. His medications were renewed. As far as food was concerned, he now had to choose from low glycemic foods and eat at least five times a day to avoid sugar lows. White rice and maida (refined flour) were completely out. Fried foods, except on occasion, were also to be avoided. He had to tweak his social life and going out drinking with friends had to be cut down.

When I saw him three weeks later, he had made

remarkable improvement. His weight had dropped by 6 kg. Sometimes a patient on the higher end of the weight scale drops weight faster at the initial stage. So, I was not worried about this huge drop in weight. He only drank alcohol once a week now and was trying to quit smoking. He handled his evening snacks the way I had explained to him—no more cookies or samosa for tea time.

In the next follow-up meet, I adjusted the doses of his medication, adjusted the diet as per his favourite foods, but emphasis was laid on portion control. He had been losing 2-3 kg a week and had lost about 12 kg in almost two months without feeling tired. He had started walking. I didn't advise him to join a gym yet, since he needed to just be active and try and lose weight first. Sometimes, people who are very overweight need to go easy on gyms seeing as chances of injuries are higher for them. They also need to relearn how to eat and manage their food. It was a long-term plan for him, so cutting back on major food groups was not advisable. This man had to lose 40 kg, and so he needed to eat well and not fall off the wagon. Once he hit a weight below 100 kg, I would allow him to go join a gym and start working out under a trained professional.

His journey is ongoing. The baby has arrived, so his motivation to improve his health is tremendous. I wish him all the luck.

ii. Thyroid

Thyroid is a hormone secreted from the thyroid gland located in the neck area. The low production of the thyroid hormone is a condition called hypothyroidism.

This deficiency is associated with weight gain and many other related issues.

Let me give you a little insight into what the thyroid hormone does. It regulates metabolic rate, body temperature, fertility, digestion, mood and memory, amongst many other processes in the body.

A few causes of thyroid irregularities are:

Toxins
Dieting
Genetics
Menopause
Vitamin deficiencies
Excess iodine
Some medications

I will only discuss hypothyroidism, and not hyperthyroidism, as it is very common in my patient population.

Some signs of hypothyroidism are:

Unusual skin and hair dryness
Weight gain
Depression
Fatigue
Heavy periods
Menstrual irregularity
Sleep disturbance
Forgetfulness
Constipation

If you have any of these symptoms, visit your doctor and

get yourself checked for hypothyroidism.

iii. Estrogen

Estrogen, also known as the female hormone, plays a major role in bone density, fat metabolism, heart function, memory and digestion. Estrogen is produced in ovaries, fat tissue and placenta. There are three kinds of estrogen—

- Estradiol:
  Estradiol is a protective estrogen which safeguards us from any damage to our hearts, bones, brain, menstrual cycle regulation, smooth skin, etc.
- Estrone:
  Estrone is produced in the fat cells and adrenal glands and is the dominant hormone after estradiol. It is decreased post-menopause. It can cause belly fat to increase, as it converts from estradiol.
- Estriol:
  Estriol is produced in the placenta during pregnancy and has been used topically to reduce symptoms of menopause.

Some causes of estrogen disturbances are:

Birth-control pills
Environmental toxin
Stress
Excessive fat

Lack of estradiol causes:

Hot flashes in menopausal women

Insulin resistance
Increased blood pressure
Increase in bad cholesterol
Hunger pangs
Skin wrinkles due to lack of collagen
Weight gain

Estrogens can be good as well as bad. On this note, we should be familiar with certain terms such as **xenoestrogens** and **phytoestrogens**.

Xenoestrogen comes from toxins in the environment, such as pesticides, plastic and food additives. You must avoid the use of plastic bottles, especially if you have left them unused for a long time. Instead, you should get stainless steel or glass bottles.

Phytoestrogens are good hormones to have and are present in plant sources or foods such as flaxseeds and soy.

iv. Progesterone

Progesterone is produced from the unfertilized egg in the ovary, and helps balance estrogen. It is also called the pregnancy hormone. Research shows that progesterone is important for breast health as well as cardiac and nervous systems. During menopause, when progesterone drops, there are symptoms like anxiety, insomnia and reduced memory.

Some causes of progesterone imbalance are:

Birth control pills
Insulin resistance

Environmental toxins
Smoking
Stress
Excessive body fat

Some signs of progesterone deficiency are:

Increase in abdominal girth (estrogen dominance)
Carbohydrate craving
Decreased libido
Depression
Dry hair
PMS or PMDD (premenstrual dysmorphic disorder)
Menstrual irregularities

v. Testosterone

Testosterone is produced from the testes in males, ovaries in females and adrenals (the small glands located above the kidneys) in both sexes.

It is a sex hormone for men that gradually decreases with age, resulting in andropause—which is similar to menopause in woman.

Irregularities in testosterone can be caused by:

Advanced age
Sedentary lifestyle
Obesity
Diabetes
Insulin resistance
Steroid intake
Pituitary gland tumour

Some of the signs to look out for are:

Increase abdominal girth
Decreased libido
Depression
Erectile dysfunction
Fatigue
Loss of muscles
Decreased bone density

vi. DHEA: Dehydroepiandrosterone

DHEA is produced from testosterone and adrenal glands and is the mother of all hormones. It helps us live longer and may help in preventing breast cancer, cardiovascular disease, osteoporosis and retaining active brain function.

Irregularity of DHEA can be caused by:

Ageing
Excessive body fat
Diabetes
Sedentary lifestyle
Steroid use
Stress

Some signs of lack of DHEA are:

Loss of libido
Increased body weight
Anxiety
Fatigue
Muscle loss

Decreased bone density
Increased abdominal girth

vii. Cortisol

Cortisol is produced from the adrenal cortex, which is the outer part of the adrenal glands. It is basically a hormone that is produced during stress.

Some medical issues associated with cortisol imbalance are:

Addison's disease
Adrenal insufficiency
Cushing syndrome
Diabetes
Hirsutism

Common causes of cortisol imbalance are:

Anger
Stress
Conflict
Fear
Depression
Starvation diets
Too much caffeine
Too much sugar in diet
Meal skipping
Lack of sleep

Some signs of excess cortisol are:

Carbohydrate cravings
Increased fat craving

Fat storage mainly around the abdomen
High triglycerides
Decreased bone density
Easy bruising
High blood sugar
Weight loss resistance
High blood pressure
Irregular periods

viii. Epinephrine and Norepinephrine

These are secreted from the adrenal glands during stress—mental or physical. They hamper glucose metabolism and increase heart rate and blood pressure, and along with another hormone, glucagon, are responsible for the breakdown of glycogen (which is a form of stored carbohydrate, that is broken down into glucose) in the liver, thus causing an increase in blood sugar levels.

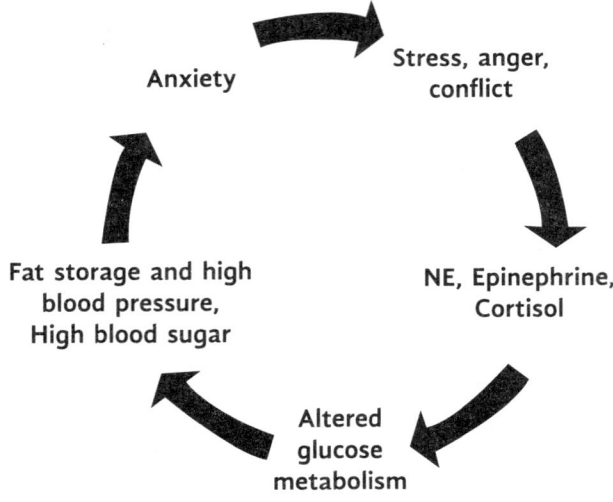

Anxiety

Stress, anger, conflict

NE, Epinephrine, Cortisol

Altered glucose metabolism

Fat storage and high blood pressure, High blood sugar

Adrenal fatigue is a term not defined by medical science, but is recognized and treated by alternative medicine. It means overstimulation and constant stimulation of adrenal glands which can lead to strokes, diabetes, heart disease etc. It can be treated by certain lifestyle modifications.

ix. Growth Hormone:

Growth hormones are produced by the pituitary gland located in the brain. They play a role in fat metabolism, preserving muscle mass. They also help to burn fat and protect the heart.

Some causes that can lead to growth hormone deficiency are:

Environmental toxins
Late nights
Sedentary lifestyle
Stress
High sugar diet
Processed carbohydrates

Signs of growth hormone deficiency are:

Delayed growth in teenagers
Dwarfism
Decrease in bone mass as age progresses
Decreased energy
Increased fat storage
Decrease in muscle mass

Taking growth hormones without proper supervision can prove detrimental to health. The idea is to preserve growth hormone production. The growth hormone is mainly secreted during deep sleep; if you are sleep deprived for any reason, the growth hormone levels will fall.

Consuming foods with high sugar or processed carbohydrates and lack of exercise will also cause a decrease in the secretion of growth hormone. Excessive exercise with no breaks can also lead to low production of growth hormone. However, the consumption of good quality protein can enhance the production of growth hormone.

x. Leptin:

Did you know that fat cells can form protein? Yes, and that protein is called leptin. Leptin works in conjunction with

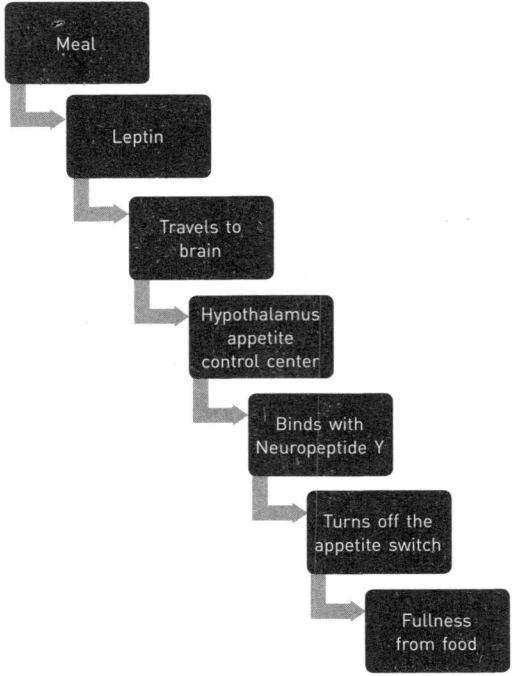

other hormones like thyroid, cortisol and insulin to control hunger.

When you eat a meal, fat cells release leptin, and that signals the hypothalamus to switch off the appetite via Neuropeptide Y. This is when we feel full.

xi. Ghrelin

Known as the hunger hormone, ghrelin produces the feeling of being hungry. It is an amino acid secreted from the stomach which influences growth hormone secretion and creates this amazing connection between the gastrointestinal system and pituitary glands (in the brain).

It is produced by epsilon cells in the stomach and the pancreas.

If you think of food, you activate ghrelin. It then signals the hypothalamic appetite centre and turns on the neuropeptide and that leads to increased appetite.

What increases ghrelin? And where can we go wrong?

High fat and sugar diet
Highly restrictive diets for too long
Low protein intake
Stress
Lack of sleep

How to fix it?

Good sleep
Last meal at 8 p.m.
Good quality protein
Eating at four hour intervals

xii. Adiponectin

Adipocyte is a specific type of protein hormone which helps in regulating glucose levels, as well as in the breakdown of fatty acids. It is reduced if one has more visceral fat (fat around the organs)—which has a close connection to insulin sensitivity and diabetes. It causes increased breakdown of fat into fatty acid and inhibits glucose production from the liver.

However, adipocytes can be increased by exercise and certain medications prescribed by a medical professional.

Let us now talk a little about CCK, PYY and GLP-1.

CCK is also known as cholecystokinin and is a hormone that is secreted in the small intestine after you have eaten a balanced meal. It tells your body to stop feeling hungry and keeps you full for three hours or so, depending on how balanced the meal was, such as a meal that is complete with fibre, protein and complex carbohydrate.

PYY is a hormone that decreases your appetite after a meal, as your stomach is stretched. Let me put it this way—what you put in your stomach bag is up to you, but once it is fully stretched, your body stops feeling hungry.

GLP-1 is a hormone that is secreted in the small intestine. It increases insulin release and delays the digestion of food, so you can be full sooner. There are mediations called GLP-1 agonists which are helpful in weight loss. It would be a good idea to talk to your doctor about these if you are suffering from obesity.

Medications and gastric bypass surgery influence these hormones and play a part in weight loss. You must visit your doctor to get more information on the hormones mentioned in this book.

6. How do you jumpstart your machine?

What is most important for starting your fitness journey and losing weight is to ask yourself *why* you want to do it. What's your motivation? Could it be an upcoming event, a new relationship/engagement, health risks, etc.?

The important part is to set a goal: whether it is weight loss or fat loss, increasing endurance and core strength, or just toning up. Start that weight loss programme by following these steps:

a. Get a diary.
b. Write down your goal, current weight, timelines, body fat percentage, measurements of your waist at the navel, your thighs, both upper and lower, your arms at the bicep level, hip circumference, and your BMI.
c. See what tools you have available to facilitate you on this journey. Can you afford a trainer at a nearby gym? Can you run/walk outdoors or do you have a cardio machine at home? Have you done your yearly physical check-up with a doctor?

Once you figure out the tools at your disposal, start a three month programme. You have to give yourself three-months and have patience to see good results. After all, that fat in your body didn't store up in just three months; it is the result of years of incorrect eating habits and little activity. However, you must keep in mind that it is never too late to begin your fitness journey.

Setting a realistic goal early on is important. If you are morbidly obese, target for merely obese, and if you are obese, target for overweight. If you are overweight, then you must try to get lean.

There is no one rule that applies to all; we are all different, with cultural differences in our lifestyles and eating habits. Therefore, it is best to stick to the food that you like and are used to eating, and make the best of it.

7. Do you need to compensate for the extra food you eat?

In my experience, this can work occasionally, but you have to learn the right way to do it—one that suits your body. Sometimes, we eat more than we should. In such cases, we can eat less in the next meal, or fast longer the next day, or exercise a little more. However, the last option rarely works. Exercise should not be treated like a punishment, and we can never burn as many calories as we ate just by exercising. For example, if you do an average intensive workout, you can burn approximately 300-400 calories, but most meals are usually much higher in calories. So, the law of compensation is usually not valid in these instances.

Fasting longer the next day can be very beneficial, and people who fast longer burn more fat. Intermittent fasting can be done by fasting continuously for 14-16 hours, or by fasting on alternate days. So, you basically have a limited window in which you can eat, and you should obviously eat healthy during this time period. In case of macros, this is more flexible than for other stricter diets and compensations. However, I suggest you first see your doctor before you fast and find out whether fasting is suitable for you, as fasting can be detrimental for people with gastric ulcers and diabetes.

There are certain quick methods of compensation, which lack any scientific backing but can work in real life.

i. Going on a protein-sparing fast, where you eat only proteins in all three meals for two or three days. However, the downside is that you might get very constipated due to the lack of fibre.

ii. Exercising more than usual—doing High-Intensity Interval Training (HIIT) workouts to burn more fat. This leads to a quick breakdown of fat to form fatty acids, which enhances the fat loss.

iii. Eating fewer calories for a couple of days. There is no downside, but hunger can kick in and make you 'hangry'—an urban term for when you get angry because of your hunger.

iv. Going on a vegetable juice fast for a day. However, these kinds of compensation require massive will power and are bad ideas if you are diabetic.

v. Sleeping it off. Not everyone will have that luxury, but if you can take it easy for the next day, go to a spa, sleep or meditate the day after you go all out on the food.

8. Is it fashionable to be thin?

Yes and no, depending on your exposure to social media. It is understandable that if you are a model or an actress, you are under greater pressure to look and measure a certain way. However, if you are not from that industry and you still take that pressure due to your peers or the prevalent societal norms, then it's not very healthy.

When we are younger, we are extremely active and we burn most of our calorie intake. However, when we start ageing, we start gaining weight, as our level of activity goes down along with a 2 per cent increase in weight with each decade that is added. When we turn 40, we might suddenly notice our tummy bulging a little more and we might accumulate fat in areas we never had before. At this age, hormonal changes, lack of enough physical activity and eating the same portions that we did when we were younger will add to it, making it look like an irreversible change. It doesn't have to be so.

In ancient times, women who were older either worked a lot till their 70s or 80s, or had very limited food. Eating food should be in accordance with the energy expended. The simple theory of calories in and calories out can work sometimes, but in this case, age must be accounted for. If you can work out, then that's the best thing to do— as that will also strengthen your bones and enhance the hormones that are slowly being depleted by the natural process of ageing.

In all of this, eating smartly, not skimpily, is important. If you can simply maintain a certain weight after 40, that's more than enough. It is certainly challenging—but easy if you have a balanced lifestyle that includes some exercise and activity. We must change the way we eat as per the needs of our body and our age. We should aspire to be healthy, and not skinny. Unfortunately, all of us look at magazines and want to be like the models without realizing that the pictures are photoshopped. What we cannot see is the harsh reality of stretch marks and blemishes and cellulite—things that all of us have, but are edited out in those photos. I have seen these people closely and they don't look the same in reality. Models and actors are real people like you and me, but they have an entourage to make them look good. We must stop aping the idea of looking perfect and try to be content with our bodies and live healthily and happily.

Case study of a real housewife in New Delhi

My most interesting patients are the housewives. They might not have a traditional workplace, but no one is as busy as them. They do a thankless job while being unappreciated, even by their own family, most of the time. They know best how they handle their homes and their social lives and therefore, it is up to them how they utilize any remaining time they have for their own health.

Let me tell you about one such magnificent woman's weight loss journey. She came to me at a time when she had huge motivation to lose weight. It was summer and she was looking forward to her daughter's wedding. Needless to say, she had to now go shopping every other day for the wedding preparations. The challenge, however, was the history of migraine that she had. She informed me that she could not create a deficit in her food; she had to eat well, or she would get migraines. But she also wanted to lose weight. This is one of those difficult scenarios that my patients sometimes approach me with. They always tell me that they have visited many nutritionists but eventually came to me because I never make my patients starve in order to get quick results. It is, indeed, a lovely compliment, but if someone is not overweight to begin with, it is challenging to help them lose weight without creating some calorie deficit—especially since most patients of mine don't want to exercise, or have never exercised before. Not that exercise is of primary importance for weight loss, but it improves insulin sensitivity in the body.

Age: 49

Sex: F

Weight: 74.3 kg

BMI: 28.3

Max weight till date: 75 kg

Min weight in the last five years: 68 kg

Previous medical issues: Hypothyroid, gall bladder removed, hx (medical history) of gastric ulcer treated, migraine, bloating, insomnia, iron deficiency, Vitamin D deficiency, menopausal, hx of spine fracture which had her bedridden for a few months and that is when she gained most of her weight

Exercise status: Swims daily, gym sometimes

Diet recall: Vegetarian but eats eggs

Breakfast: Milk and fruit

Lunch: Roti, sabzi and salad

Evening snacks: Cookies or namkeen

Dinner: Soup or milk with fruits

Social history: No alcohol or smoking

Sleep: 5-6 hours

Water intake: Not a big fan of drinking water

Supplements: None

Medications: For hypothyroid; painkiller for migraine attacks (class of NSAID)

Plan: First things first, she needed to stop taking painkillers of the NSAID variety, as they cause many health repercussions such as kidney disease and gastritis; she already had a history of gastric ulcer.

I started her on migraine prophylaxis medication along with Vitamin B6 so that her attacks were reduced in frequency and were also less intense.

She was provided with iron and Vitamin D supplements as well.

She needed to cut back on milk, bread, maida (refined flour), onions, sweets, ginger, biscuits and namkeen for two reasons—one, they are potential migraine onset offenders and two, they are also high calorie snacks that are a deterrent to weight loss and cause bloating.

Her initial weight loss started very easily when she gave up the forbidden foods.

As she had a history of vitamin deficiency, the plan had to be highly nutritive, even though I created a calorie deficit.

If you see her diet recall, you will notice the exact cause of her bloating—milk and fruits twice a day as substitute for meals. That is poor eating habit, as no real food was being consumed by her.

She had been having salad for lunch but since she had to go out regularly, it was difficult for her to manage. Therefore, I gave her besan (chickpea flour) rotis stuffed with spinach, which she could pack and thus not have junk food during her outings. However, she had to start with a nutritive and large breakfast so that she didn't get too hungry too soon. I gave her eggs, except for Tuesday and Thursday, along with a complex carb—like oatmeal. She was also given the option of oatmeal cooked with salt and vegetables. This type of breakfast keeps you full for longer. I also advised her to have some fruit every two hours, and to carry nuts for any hunger pangs.

Her evening snack was another issue. Since she was going to be out, I couldn't possibly ask her to carry so much food during summer in India. I asked her to buy some healthy snacks like pumpkin seeds, lotus seeds and flaxseeds and keep them handy—packaged food that doesn't get spoiled.

Interestingly, she had been to a dietician for help with weight loss. She was taken off salt and developed even greater hypothyroidism as a result. You see, salt is the only source of good quality iodine in vegetarian diets and if you restrict that without having a history of high blood pressure, your thyroid gland will get affected—as iodine is very necessary for conversion of T4 (the pill) to the active form of thyroid hormone, T3. The conversion of T4 to T3 is affected by lack of nutrients, vitamins and micro elements like iodine, selenium and iron.

I asked her to continue with my plan for at least two

months. Since it was a well-balanced plan, I could easily see her at longer intervals. When she came back at the end of one-and-a-half months, she had lost 5 kg without feeling like she was on a diet. I changed her plan and included lentils and more vegetarian options for her. At that pace, she was set to lose 2 kg every month; her current weight, after six months, is 63 kg. She has lost about 11 kg slowly and steadily. Her migraines are better and I asked her to contact her neurologist for further treatment and maintenance of her migraine medication. She wants to lose more weight, but that may show on her face through sunken eyes and in other ways. It took a lot of convincing, but now she is on a simple routine for weight maintenance.

Now, it is important that you eat what you like at least two to three times a week. Giving up on a certain food type is the worst thing we can do to our body, since our mood is heavily influenced by the food we eat. Don't you feel irritated when someone doesn't give you food on time, or you go hungry for a very long time? If someone gives me bland food, I get really upset—and I understand that it is the same with my patients. Food needs to have flavour and taste. As per Ayurveda, any given food should have five flavours to be satisfying. If you are not satisfied, you will hunt for other food that will make you content. The six flavours are: sweet, salty, sour, pungent, bitter and astringent. How closely your food resembles these flavours is the secret of satisfaction. Food has to satisfy the soul too. So, staying close to these basic flavours and getting them all in the right proportion is the trick. There is food available for every mood. For instance, we can use sweet potatoes to reduce anxiety, egg yolk for good concentration, fatty acids for improved communication between brain and body, mushrooms to boost immunity, and saffron to make us happy. One must not completely curb their cravings. However, in the process of satisfying our cravings, we must not end up overeating.

Just as in your daily life you need a good weekend to make yourself feel happy and fresh, in the same way, our body also needs some changes in the food we eat to keep it happy and healthy. If a person is feeling sad and depressed, then he/she should have the foods which regulate their serotonin—a chemical produced in the nerve cells, that plays a major role in producing happy and relaxed feelings. A food that contains tryptophan and amino acids is really effective for good mood, because they are really good at maintaining the serotonin levels in our brain. Serotonin is also good for good sleep and it regulates appetite and helps us relax.

As per the requirements of the clients, food should have flavours and must be interesting. If food is not tasty and flavourful, people will not feel like consuming it and might even lean towards unhealthy food. Unhealthy food items look good but are not good for your health. Unhappy people often go after food that looks nice and tasty, like ice cream, pasta, potatoes and various junk foods. So, while thinking about their health and mood—which basically depends on food—we should not forget that certain foods have negative effects as well. It is thought that eating fruits, vegetables and nuts make you happier. Banana is also considered a happy food, because it has tryptophan. Healthy, colourful, tasty and clean food also helps keep the gut healthy and the brain functioning. The brain is connected to the gut and if the gut is healthy, the person will also feel healthy. The opposite is also true—an unhealthy gut might lead to mood swings and depression.

Eating bad fats leads to depression and therefore, we must avoid trans fats and go for unsaturated fats. Foods like milk and milk products, meat and packaged foods contain trans fats. There are some nutrients which play a very important role in mood regulation, for e.g., omega fatty acids, selenium, Vitamin D, magnesium, Vitamin B12 and folic acid. A good source of omega fatty acids is fish.

You should always make changes and introduce new food products in your diet, but you should avoid sugary items and processed foods, because these items cause more food cravings—which might lead to you eating unhealthy food.

How closely your food contains all the five flavours is the secret of food satisfaction. Your food should be balanced in the matter of taste and quantity. Some people like having sugar, but as shown above, having too much sugar is not advisable. Try to have natural flavours over artificial ones. Instead of processed sugar, you should use either natural sugar like dates, figs, fruits, coconut sugar, palm sugar or sweeteners which are not harmful to health. One can have their favourite kheer, ice cream or custard with natural sugar. Anyone who is suffering from hypertension and wants to have a good amount of salt in their food can have rock salt or low sodium salt; for bitter flavours, you can use cider or lemon; for pungency, you can use mustard or ginger; and for astringent quality, you can use onions or garlic.

So, in order to feel motivated, you should eat a protein-rich, colourful, nutrient-rich and well-balanced diet.

Chapter 2

Balancing Health and Taste

In this chapter, I shall discuss the most important aspects of nutrition optimization, and how you can best balance nutrition and taste in your food.

1. Eating whole foods

A lot of times, I get this question: what exactly is a 'whole food'? Anything that is not overly processed is a whole food. When a food is 'processed', it means that it goes through many changes (in a factory) before being brought to the store shelf.

Let me give you an example. White bleached flour, which we call 'maida', is a good example of overly processed wheat—whole wheat is wheat that has been ground with all its parts intact, like its outer covering, which is usually separately sold in stores as bran. All other grains have similar examples.

Whole foods also include whole vegetables, whole dairy, whole fruits and whole nuts.

Some examples of whole foods, apart from whole

wheat, are brown raw sugar, real fruits with edible peels and not dried candied fruits, vegetables and not vegetable chips, lentils that have their covers intact and have not been processed etc.

2. Knowing how to read a glycemic index

It can be very beneficial for diabetics, as well as people trying to lose weight in general, to choose their food by reading the glycemic index number on its label. The smaller the number, the lesser the effect the food has on your blood sugar.

Food	Glycemic index number	Quantity
OATS	58	1 CUP
WHITE RICE	64	1 CUP
BROWN RICE	55	1 CUP
WHITE BREAD	70	1 SLICE
LENTILS	29	1 CUP
WHOLE WHEAT ROTI	62	1 CUP
POP CORN	72	1 CUP
CHICK PEAS	31	1 CUP
RAJMA	28	1 CUP
APPLE	38	1 MEDIUM
BANANA	52	1 LARGE
MANGO	51	1 CUP
GREEN BEANS	0	
GOURD (GHIYA)	0	
ORANGE JUICE	57	1 CUP
CABBAGE	0	

BROCCOLI	0	
CAULIFLOWER	0	
FROZEN PEAS	50	½ CUP
WATER MELON	55	1 CUP
JAMUN	10	1 CUP
LADIES' FINGER (BHINDI)	10	1 CUP
WHOLE MILK	40	1 CUP
PLAIN YOGHURT	36	1 CUP
SOY MILK	44	1 CUP
COLA	63	1 CUP
BOILED POTATO	51	1 CUP
LOW FAT PANEER	35	150 GM
FISH	0	
CHICKEN	0	
PRAWN	0	

3. Calories and beyond

When it comes to our health and staying fit, we should opt for caloric balance in our routine. But how many of us actually know how to have caloric balance in our diets? Instead, we turn calorie counting into a game.

We all know a balanced diet is helpful for maintaining a healthy lifestyle. If you are on a weight loss journey, calorie counting may help you in rapid weight loss and you may achieve your goals. However, if you are thinking of continuing for a long period of time, you may find calorie counting tedious and often incorrect. Calorie counting can never be accurate; it is always an estimation to keep yourself roughly in check, so you don't eat anything extra.

a. We seldom practice balance in calories: We must focus more on how to burn calories, rather than getting worked up over calorie consumption.

Why get worried if you are eating a piece of cake or a sweet when you are having your 'cheat' meal? Instead, think of a physical activity or try to complete your fitness plan the next day, which will refresh you and help with the guilt.

Sometimes, we are unable to balance our calories as the consumption of calories, intentionally or unintentionally, overtakes their expenditure. If you are overweight, it means that you are ingesting more calories than you need and adding unwanted body fat (as these excess calories are stored in your adipose tissue).

b. Negative energy balance is not good for us in the long run: This might seem very helpful during your weight loss regimen, as you can shed the unwanted weight gradually. However, if you practice this over a long period without considering your nutritional needs—like your intake of calories from protein, carbohydrate, fats, vitamin and minerals—you may experience health issues. For maintaining overall fitness, health and well-being, a caloric balance matters.

c. We are least interested in the type of calorie we ingest: It is really important to choose our meal carefully and know what types of calories it holds. Calories from protein and from carbohydrates will have different roles and benefits.

Protein: Taking calories from protein will help in reducing appetite, as protein intake stimulates the production of hormones that do so (as mentioned before). This will help you avoid bingeing every now and then.

Carbohydrate: If you are eating a combination of carbs and fat, it will boost the stimulation of triglycerides—which needs medical attention. Taking calories from carbohydrates will also stimulate the production of insulin, which will reduce the body's ability to burn fat, leading to increased fat storage in the body.

d. Let it be a mind game: A low calorie diet will help you for a short while, when you want to lose weight rapidly. But in the long run, you can use these tips to play games with your mind.

1. Drink plenty of water and alternate alcohol with chilled water.
2. Delight yourself with a plate of proteins for your breakfast.
3. To control bingeing, keep yourself busy with work or hang on to your hobbies.
4. Make a factual plan for a fitness regime.
5. Avoid midnight snacking. Instead, choose fibre-rich food for your plate.
6. Choosing the right exercise pattern is very important.
7. Stick with small portions of multiple meals rather than choosing a heavy meal twice a day.
8. Eat your calories rather than drinking them, or

alternate them with fruit juices and other non-alcoholic drinks.

4. Nutrients and supplements

a. Complex carbohydrates and simple carbohydrates

Carbohydrates are in everything that we eat, except lean proteins coming from animals and water. They can be easily classified into 'complex' and 'simple'.

Complex carbohydrates are hard for the body to break down. The process takes time, so they keep you full for longer. Simple carbohydrates need no digestion and can be absorbed by the system as they are. They leave the stomach so fast that before you realize it, you are already hungry.

Examples of complex carbohydrate are whole grains, vegetables, fruits, beans, lentils, and peas. They give you sustained energy and keep you full for longer; they are also good for your bowel movement. They are important for good sleep and brain function.

Simple carbohydrates are table sugar, fruit juices, sauces, candies, sugary chocolates, jams, jellies, corn syrup, sugar syrup, artificial pancake syrup, all sweets etc. If you can avoid them, you must; but if you cannot, then at least try to reduce the intake.

Have you ever felt even hungrier after a slice of cake? Or a scoop of ice cream? This is because carbs attract carbs. You must always remember this.

b. Proteins: The building blocks

Proteins are made of amino acids and are required by every cell in our bodies, for self-repair and generation of new ones. That's why they are called the building blocks of our body.

There are essential and non-essential amino acids. We have to get essential amino acids from food, as our bodies cannot make it. However, non-essential amino acids are made inside the body.

Protein in the diet should be around 10-35 per cent, depending on the weight and height. For a 2000 calorie diet, protein intake should be 80-90 gm approximately. Many people consider this a high amount of protein and label such a diet a high-protein diet. However, I have observed that not everyone eats the right amount of protein.

Beneficial effects of proteins:

Protein has had a bad rap due to people going on high protein diets; protein portions are highly misunderstood by the majority of people. Balancing nutrients is important and so you should take the help of a well-qualified nutritionist to meet your protein needs per day.

If you are working out in a gym or are an athlete, the protein needs of your body increase depending on your body weight.

Everything is made from protein in our bodies. Hair, skin, nails, immune system, cell repair—everything depends on proteins. I have seen people go on starvation diets and then come to me and complain that their hair is falling out, or their nails break easily, or that they feel tired all the time, etc. When I do a diet recall, I don't see any protein intake.

Vegetarians think that dals/legumes make them fat and so they don't eat them. It is not the lentils that can make you fat—it is the Indian style tadka in it that makes it hard to lose weight due to the increase in calories.

Proteins are underutilized or over-utilized in most Indian diets. All proteins are not created equal. Vegetarian proteins are non-lean proteins and non-vegetarian proteins are lean proteins. Vegetarian proteins come from soy, legumes, nut butters, wheat germ, quinoa etc. Animal proteins come from meat, fish, eggs, milk etc. Animal sources provide the amino acids we need. Other foods lack one or two amino acids. This is important for those who have diabetes or are at a risk of it.

Healthy sources of proteins include:

i.   Lean chicken/meat/fish/shellfish/egg whites
ii.   Beans: red kidney beans, chickpeas, lentils, split peas. Chickpeas also have high amounts of carbs. So they are good for a maintenance diet. Same is the case with lentils (dals), sprouted or dried. They are better than gobbling up any other fried or sweet food.
iii. Nuts
iv.   Soy: tofu, tempeh, edamame. For the Indian palate, I suggest tofu, cooked like our matar paneer.
v.   Cottage cheese (paneer)/ricotta cheese or Greek yoghurt.

vi. You can buy low carb protein powder and make a couple of low carb protein smoothies at home with antioxidant berries.

vii. Milk has about 7 gm of protein per cup. People with lactose intolerance can get soy milk, which has the same protein content.

viii. Mushroom

ix. Soybeans

x. Peanut butter and almond butter

xi. Coconut

xii. Curd/hung curd/chaach

xiii. Chia/hemp/pumpkin seeds

xiv. Barley

xv. Broccoli

xvi. Cauliflower

xvii. Sweet corn

c. Fats

Eliminate the term 'fat-free'. Fats are an essential part of our diet. It is best to not believe everything written on the web or magazines and follow those suggestions blindly. What you must know is that all fat is not bad, but excess of any fat is bad.

Fat provides 9 calories per gram. A 2000 calorie diet should have 400 calories or 144 gm of fat, which is roughly around 44-78 gm of fat per day. However, the latest dietary recommendation from the American Heart Association is to keep saturated fat to less than 10 per cent of the total calorie intake. So, a 2000-calorie diet should have 200 calories or 22 grams of fat.

Fats can be classified as good fats and bad fats. Good fats are mono-saturated fatty acids (MUFA) and polyunsaturated fatty acids (PUFA). Some examples of good fats are olive oil, canola oil, sunflower oil, soy, corn oil etc. These may help lower LDL, the bad cholesterol which can lead to heart attack, and increase the scavenger HDL, the good cholesterol which protects the heart.

Bad fats are also called trans fats. Processed foods contain trans fats like partially hydrogenated fats.

Cooking only in olive oil, however, need not necessarily be healthy if you are using a lot of it. Upon heating, most oils can turn into trans fats—so you have to be careful when frying in oil. I advise most of my patients to try to make reading labels a habit, to find out what kind of fat you are consuming.

Saturated fats found in meat, butter, and cheeses are not very harmful.

Fat	Per cent Saturated fat
Canola oil	7
Sunflower oil	12
Sesame oil	10
Corn oil	13
Olive oil	15
Soybean oil	15
Peanut oil	19
Butter	68
Coconut oil	91
Ghee	75

d. Vitamins and minerals

The following are the important vitamins, minerals and supplements for weight loss and longevity.

I. Vitamins

a. Vitamin B12

Vitamin B12 is a weight loss vitamin that is especially recommended for vegetarians, because they tend to have lower values of Vitamin B12 than the non-vegetarian population. Vitamin B12 is essential for weight loss because it is a cofactor which is essential for the functioning of important enzymes of metabolism. It also reduces the risk of macro degeneration (damage to the macula, which is the small central area on the retina of the eye and is responsible for vision) and memory loss, and helps in proper cardiac functioning leading to a healthy heart. Apart from boosting metabolism and the correction of underlying deficiencies, Vitamin B12 will increase your energy levels, thus making you more active and further helping in weight loss.

Who's at risk of Vitamin B12 deficiency?

People who have had gastric bypass surgery or any gastro-intestinal surgery; people who don't absorb nutrients well, like patients with celiac disease or Crohn's disease.

Symptoms of Vitamin B12 deficiency:

Nerve pain (especially in the arms or legs)

Lethargy
Weight gain
Tingling sensation in feet

Dosage:

Start with 500 mcg. Get your B12 levels tested before starting supplementation, so you can build it up and then recheck levels in about two months. During pregnancy, the dosage needs to be increased and adjusted by your doctor. This vitamin is also available in an injectable form. If a patient has really low values, we start with injections and then maintain them through oral medication. It is also a water soluble vitamin that does not necessarily need to be had with food.

Some sources of Vitamin B12 are:

Shellfish
Meat and poultry
Eggs
Plant milks fortified with B12
Nutritional yeast
Fortified cereals

b. Vitamin B6

Vitamin B6, also known as pyridoxine, is another water soluble vitamin. It is essential for weight loss and mental well-being, and is also used during the treatment of tuberculosis. Vitamin B6 supports adrenal function and is very important for metabolic processes. It helps in the breakdown of carbohydrate, fat and protein. It also helps in the production of neurotransmitters. It is extremely beneficial for Premenstrual Syndrome (PMS), memory loss, diabetes, asthma, Attention Deficit Hyperactivity Disorder (ADHD), lung cancer, acne, kidney stones, Polycystic Ovarian Syndrome (PCOS) and depression.

Symptoms of Vitamin B6 deficiency:

Hyperthyroidism, dermatitis, cracked lips, inflamed tongue, depression, insomnia

Dosage:

Recommendation is 1.3 mg for all adults between 19-50. The need will increase during pregnancy and lactation. I use about 5-10 mg a day, for a few days in a month.

Some sources of Vitamin B6 are:

Bananas
Brewer's yeast
Legumes (dals)
Spinach
Carrot
Peas
Cheese
Eggs
Fish
Seeds

Some other B vitamins are as follows:

- B3 is excellent for reducing cholesterol, especially if you have elevated triglycerides.
- B1 is essential for people who like alcohol or have a poor appetite, diarrhea, inflammatory bowel disease or canker sores (mouth ulcers). Deficiency can cause serious problems such as a nervous problem called Wernike Korsakoff syndrome. A good multivitamin will help, along with a healthy diet.
- Riboflavin or B2 is a great vitamin for migraines, burning feet and acne. It increases iron absorption in the body. It can be found in meat, vegetables, nuts, eggs, etc.
- B5 or pantothenic acids are used for good skin, ADHD, baldness, asthma, arthritis and muscle dystrophies. There haven't been enough studies to warrant the above benefits, but B5 is usually present in all multivitamins. It can be found in the same sources as riboflavin.
- Vitamin B7, also called Biotin, is great for hair and nails as well as hormone synthesis.
- I believe everyone knows about Vitamin B9 or folate, which is very essential for all women who intend to have children, to prevent developmental anomalies in the babies in the womb. These vitamins are also used to maintain DNA and red blood cells. Alcoholics, people with poor appetite, pregnant women or women who wish to become pregnant need an extra 1 mg of B9 per day.

c. Vitamin D

Vitamin D is a fat soluble vitamin derived from food and sunlight. A lot of research has been done relating Vitamin D consumption to weight loss and vice versa. People who are overweight usually eat more empty calories and are inactive. They are therefore unable to get enough sunshine—so their Vitamin D level falls.

Symptoms of Vitamin D deficiency:

Depression, weight gain, aches and pains, osteoporosis, joint pain

Dosage:

As Asians, exposure to the sun for fifteen-twenty minutes, around 11 a.m., is highly beneficial for our bodies, allowing them to produce enough Vitamin D. However, if you have a family history of skin cancer, limit your exposure to the sun. Dosage is anywhere from 600 IU (International Units) to 1000 IU per day, and it is to be taken under medical supervision.

Some sources of Vitamin D are:

> Fish—especially salmon, mackerel and tuna
> Red meat
> Liver
> Egg yolk and some fortified breakfast cereals
> Sunlight—Vitamin D converts to its active form in
the skin with the help of sunlight. Darker-skinned people produce less Vitamin D compared to fair-skinned people,

and are at greater risk of deficiency.

d. Vitamin C

Vitamin C is a water soluble vitamin and is an immunity booster and antioxidant.

Symptoms of Vitamin C deficiency:

Cracked lips, especially at the corners of the mouth
Burning tongue
Lethargy
Decreased muscle strength
Lustreless and wrinkly skin, easy bruising
Swollen gums
Dry hair
Nosebleeds
Red spots on skin
Weak immune system
Leaky gut
Weight gain
Painful joints
Long-term deficiency has been shown to affect the heart and brain and also cause high blood pressure.

Dosage:

Start out at 500 mg, especially if you go to the gym regularly. Take the dosage under a doctor's supervision.

Some sources of Vitamin C are:

Fruits and vegetables

II. Magnesium

Magnesium is taken in a chelated form orally. It helps in weight loss and is also great for bone health. Magnesium is also connected to other nutrients, as it helps balance out calcium in the body. Apart from causing an increase in activity level and leading to an anxiety-free life, it helps clear the stomach very well so that toxin build-up is low. My clients feel much better if they are on magnesium and therefore, are better able to absorb nutrients from the intestine.

Symptoms of magnesium deficiency:

Magnesium deficiency is common in overweight people and people who drink alcohol. So, first get your levels checked and make sure you get them replenished by a doctor. Symptoms of magnesium deficiency are aches and pain in the muscles, anxiety, poor digestion, constipation, PMS (Pre-menstrual Syndrome), osteoporosis, weak teeth, cavities and pregnancy complications.

Dosage:

I use 400 to 500 mg daily.

Some sources of magnesium are:

>   Spinach
>   Mung and other beans
>   Almonds
>   Cashews
>   Potatoes

Pumpkin seeds
Banana
Avocado
Broccoli

III. Omega 3 (fish oil)

Omega 3 (fish oil) is made of eicosapentaenoic acid (EPA) and docosahexaenoic acid (DHA). Omega 3 helps in weight loss because it reduces inflammation in the body. It also helps with depression, ADHD, memory loss, heart health, vision improvement and mental disorders.

There are no symptoms of Omega 3 deficiency.

Dosage:

Dosage is to be decided by the doctor, since there is a risk of over-ingestion of fish oils. It can also cause some indigestion and diarrhea.

Some sources of Omega 3 are:

The best source is wild Alaskan salmon. I do not recommend farm-grown salmon oil.
Flaxseeds
Hemp seed
Chia seed
Dark leafy vegetables
Spirulina
Walnuts

IV. L-carnitine

L-carnitine is an amino acid used extensively in weight loss.

Its benefits also include improving heart health and reducing pain in the body due to claudication. It is beneficial for people on medication for AIDS, chronic fatigue syndrome and ADHD. L-carnitine helps by producing energy in the body, therefore making an overweight, lethargic person active. Some studies show that it can cause increased muscle mass and reduced fat mass. Some people use it as a fat burner owing to its fat oxidizing effect.

Symptoms of L-carnitine deficiency:

Deficiency is seen in patients who are on medication for seizures or who undergo dialysis. Deficiency can also be seen in vegetarians, frequent dieters and premature infants.

Dosage:

I usually start with 500 mg a day before hitting the gym.

Some sources of L-carnitine are:

Beef
Pork/bacon
Chicken breast
Cheese
Milk
Cottage cheese
Whole wheat bread
Avocado

V. CoQ-10

CoQ-10 is an antioxidant. It prevents ageing, protects the

heart and blood vessels from free radical damage and is used to treat heart conditions and other conditions like diabetes and breast cancer. CoQ-10 also acts as a coenzyme that helps other enzymes digest food, thereby helping with the absorption of nutrients (which decreases with age).

Symptoms of CoQ-10 deficiency:

Signs of CoQ-10 deficiency include muscle weakness, fatigue, high blood pressure, decreased cognitive ability, heart arrhythmia (heart rate variations), increased or slowed heart rate, movement disorders and seizures.

Dosage:

Start with 100 mg per day. Depending on what results are to be achieved, the physician will increase or decrease the dosage. You must always consult a doctor first.

Some sources of CoQ-10 are:

Organic eggs
Strawberries
Organic chicken
Sesame seeds
Pistachios
Broccoli
Cauliflower
Orange
Certain fish

VI. MSM

I love MSM, as it is good for all ages. It is a sulphur-containing supplement that treats joint diseases, joint pains, decreases inflammation in the body, improves a leaky gut, helps to maintain the youthfulness of skin, helps in hair growth, PMS symptoms, stretch marks and oral infections.

Note: If you're allergic to sulphur drugs, then you may be allergic to MSM.

Symptoms of MSM deficiency:

Pain inflammation, digestive issues, asthma, chronic fatigue syndrome, muscle wasting diseases

Dosage:

I normally like to start my patients off at 1000 mg a day, as a pill or a powder, which can be decreased or increased depending on the effect. It should be taken under your doctor's recommendations.

Some sources of MSM are:

Cruciferous broccoli
Cabbage
Brussels sprout
Cow milk
Coffee
Legumes (dals)
Whole grains
Apples
Raspberries
Tea
Tomatoes

Garlic

Onions

Organic eggs

VII. Iodine

It is an essential trace element that is vital for normal growth and development.

Iodine controls the body's base metabolic rate and maintains optimal energy levels.

It is important for healthy and shiny skin and boosts the immune system. It also stimulates hormonal activity and is used as a cure for an enlarged thyroid gland. It prevents dangerous forms of cancer and flushes out chemical toxins.

Symptoms of iodine deficiency:

Thyroid gland enlargement, fatigue, weight gain, hair loss, dry flaky skin, cognitive dysfunction

Dosage:

Recommended dietary allowances (RDA) of iodine are as follows—

Age	Men	Female	Pregnancy	Lactation
Birth-6 months	110 mcg*	110 mcg*		
7-12 months	130 mcg*	130 mcg*		
1-3 years	90 mcg	90 mcg		
4-8 years	90 mcg	90 mcg		

9-13 years	120 mcg	120 mcg		
14-18 years	150 mcg	150 mcg	220 mcg	290 mcg
19+ years	150 mcg	150 mcg	220 mcg	290 mcg

Some sources of iodine are:

Iodine is present in large quantities in both marine plants and animals, including shellfish, deep water whitefish, and brown seaweed kelp. Dulse (a form of seaweed) also contains dietary iodine.

For vegetarians, garlic, lima beans, sesame seeds, soybeans, turnip, greens and spinach are rich in iodine. Iodized salt is another important source of iodine.

VIII. Iron

Iron is a very essential mineral. It forms haemoglobin, which women usually require more than men. Iron is of two types—heme iron and non-heme iron. Iron from meat is called heme iron and is easily absorbed. Non heme iron is present in vegetables and can't be absorbed very well. Iron plays a very important role in immunity and infections.

Symptoms of iron deficiency:

Low energy, hair thinning and loss, stunted growth in children, split nails and cold hands and feet

Dosage:

The daily requirement is 18 mg. Iron tablets should be taken with caution, as high levels can be toxic to humans. Try to take it with meals as it will reduce the side effects of an upset stomach.

Some sources of iron are:

Beef, iron-fortified cereals, potatoes, pumpkin seeds, soybeans, spinach, nuts.

Junk and packaged foods have low iron content.

IX. Probiotics and prebiotics

Probiotics are the good bacteria needed by our gut to maintain health and immunity. Probiotics can be especially useful if you are suffering from gastrointestinal issues and have undergone a prolonged use of antibiotics. The probiotic type depends upon what issue you have—so consult a doctor who can help you choose the right supplement for yourself.

Dosage:

Several billion colonies of good bacteria are used as a therapeutic dose, but you have to consult a specialist to get the right dose.

Some sources of probiotics are:

Fermented dairy—for example, kefir, chaach or buttermilk, kimchi, tempeh, yoghurt, sauerkraut, miso, kombucha, etc.

X. Stomach acids and digestive enzymes

'Stomach acid' is hydrochloric acid, which helps in the digestion of food after it reaches the stomach. If you don't have enough stomach acid, you may burp a lot. Stomach acid decreases with age as you develop an inability to digest proteins. To correct this, you can start with a tablespoon of organic apple cider vinegar diluted in a cup of water. Take it a few minutes before eating food. Or you can take an HCL supplement, but that has to be under the strict supervision of a doctor.

Digestive enzymes are important enzymes produced by the body to digest protein, carbohydrates, and fats. Sometimes we all need digestive enzymes, depending upon the symptoms we have. These can help ease bloating, gas, and heartburn, but eventually these symptoms reoccur due to eating in stress or in a hurry. Some enzymes may be lacking in the body, so we give enzyme supplements to the patients depending on what is needed. There are a lot of herbal preparations available to help ease the symptoms of indigestion via digestive enzymes.

Case study of a person facing an auto immune condition

Age: 30

Sex: M

Weight: 74 kg

BMI: 22.76

Max weight till date: 75 kg

Min weight in the last five years: 67 kg

Previous medical issues: Ocular migraine, low BP, anxiety issues, low immunity, autoimmune disorder, Vitamin D and Vitamin B12 deficiencies, disturbed sleep, bloating, fatigue, lethargy, insomnia, pain in the lower back

Exercise status: Not really, due to back pain

Diet recall: Non-vegetarian, having gluten-free diet already

Plan: I started his treatment by introducing some supplements like omega fish oil, probiotics and curcumin 500 mg to his diet. I also suggested Vitamin D and Vitamin B12 as he was deficient in them.

As per his symptoms and his autoimmune issues, I put him on an elimination diet. On this particular diet plan, he had to cut back on milk, bread, sugar, eggs, soya, tofu, butter, cheese, cottage cheese, soya milk, coconut yoghurt, mixed nuts, peanuts, peanut butter, corn, potato, mushroom, pumpkin, tomato, spinach, salsa, dried fruits, citrus fruits, cashews, sunflower seeds, walnuts and yoghurt.

I did recall his previous diet plan, but we could not find anything that was causing bloating. So, we decided to put him on an elimination diet plan to find out the real cause. I prepared a diet plan according to his weight and convenience. In this diet, during breakfast, I gave him complex carbs; for lunch, normal food items like rice, dal, chapati, vegetables and salads; and for dinner, protein with one cup of vegetables. For his morning snack, he requested us to not prescribe anything as he did not usually feel hungry at the time. As he was a working man, it was difficult to cook in the evening and so I gave him some easy-to-carry options like seed mix, chana jor, makhane, nuts, boiled channe etc. He was quite happy and satisfied with his diet plan.

He followed this diet plan for three weeks, and initially, the result was very good. After three weeks, I saw him again to check his development. Several of his symptoms, like low BP, anxiety issues and his weight gain problem had disappeared. But fatigue, lethargy and disturbed sleep were still very much there. As we had managed to remove his bloating and various other issues by giving him an elimination diet, this time we focused on his low energy and fatigue problems. His diet was going well, but he was suffering from back pain. So, I suggested boswellia extract to him, which is very good for pains and aches.

This time, we also had to focus on the calories given in the plan. It was possible that he was feeling lethargic and low on energy because of low calorie intake, so we increased the calories in his plan. He also requested me to add sweet potato in his diet plan for his evening snack. In this plan, we reintroduced some food items like spinach, quinoa, sweet potato, cashews, flaxseeds, spinach soup, kale and sabudana khichdi. Both breakfast and dinner were the same as the previous plan, but I gave new options for lunch such as quinoa salads, chole salads, brown rice with dal, sabudana khichdi, falafel, rajma and alternate flour chapati with one cup of vegetables. I also prescribed chaach as a morning snack.

I planned a well-balanced maintenance diet plan which he could follow for a longer time.

Supplements were the same as what he had been having—nothing was added or eliminated. For stress management, I suggested meditation to him for at least fifteen days, and shared some information on how to go about it.

After following this diet plan, he was satisfied. He started feeling good healthwise and all his autoimmune signs and symptoms disappeared.

XI. Adaptogens

These are perfect examples of food as medicine. We use adaptogens to protect the body from stress and increased levels of cortisol, which is a stress hormone. They also help with fatigue, hormone balance, low sex drive, low immunity, anxiety, depression, cancer etc.

Here are some examples of adaptogens. It is advisable to talk to a doctor before taking these.

1. Tulsi
2. Indian ginseng or ashwagandha
3. Astralagus root
4. Licorice or mulethi
5. Rhodiola
6. Cordyceps mushroom
7. Maca root

Chapter 3

Making Dietary Changes

In order to live a hearty, healthy life, we must make certain changes in the way we eat. The following are some of my suggestions.

1. Think global but eat local

We often have food fads where people follow certain diets from the west. We cannot just ape their foods as, first of all, those foods are super expensive, and secondly, they mostly come out of cold storage or are even genetically modified. We must stick to local produce—especially for fruits and vegetables. Nowadays, blueberries and avocados are locally produced; they may not look the same but at least they are homemade. Quinoa is being grown locally as well. Your average local vegetable vendor stocks forty to fifty different types of vegetables and you must make full use of the fact. Also, seasonal and local vegetables are well suited to our environment and our bodies. Every part of India has certain foods suited to seasons, and there are reasons for it. Our country has different climates in different zones. Because of such diversity, we have to stick to what is grown locally, as our bodies acclimatize to our environment. For example, tamarind is eaten a lot in south India as it keeps the body cool; however, the same thing, eaten in the cooler parts of the country can lead to joint pains.

2. Eating in moderation: The game changer

The success of a good health plan lies in the portion sizes. You can eat anything, but if you eat in small portions, you will not feel deprived of any kind of food. Most people give up some macronutrient or the other, and then they binge eat later. It is not advisable to do so. A meal should be balanced and well planned. If your body misses out on a nutrient, you are bound to feel hungry and eat more at some point during the day. A balanced diet for the day should have some carbs, proteins, fats, vegetables etc. You can have a chocolate once in a while, enjoy a dollop of an ice cream sometimes, or maybe even a glass of wine. You don't have to give up on the things you love. Food must satisfy the soul—whence the term 'soul food'.

3. Food portion guide

The guide to managing your food portions is a simple one. Your palm is the amount of protein you must have in your diet, your fist the amount of vegetables, your thumb the fat and the whole hand, the carb/grain. This is easy to remember and when you go out, always keep the plate method in mind. https://www.choosemyplate.gov is a good resource to look up for this.

4. Foods that help you lose weight

Fibre-rich foods, good fats and proteins are the main types of food that help you lose weight. Fibre-rich foods like vegetables, whole grains and salads keep you full and absorb bad toxins from your gut. Lack of fibre causes constipation and that, in turn, keeps the toxins circulating in the intestines, eventually getting absorbed in the blood stream—making you feel lethargic and bloated and increasing the growth of bad bacteria in the intestines. Therefore, adequate fibre is very important. Good fats like nuts, cold-pressed oils, avocados, ghee, egg yolk, cheese, fish rich in Omega 3, chia seeds, flaxseeds, pumpkin seeds and sunflower seeds are all great for losing weight. The transit time of these fats in the stomach is slow. They keep you full, act as laxatives and replace the stored bad fats, resulting in fat loss. Most people are afraid of fats when, in reality, it is fried foods one should be afraid of. Fried foods are often fried again and again in the same oil and are extremely bad for health, as they become toxic on being reheated. Proteins are excellent for losing weight; when eaten in the right amounts and under supervision, they can really help build muscle and lower fat in the body. They are excellent food for satiation. Lean proteins are often consumed for weight loss and fat loss. When you work out, you break muscle and to replenish that, you must have adequate proteins so that your body can heal itself. Otherwise, the broken muscle will not repair itself and you might end up losing a part of your metabolic hub.

5. The elixir of life—water

We all know that water is a colourless chemical substance with the basic pH (acidity) of 7. Water is the cheapest weight loss tool, because it boosts metabolism, increases energy, improves fatigue, flushes out toxins (if you are diabetic, it dilutes the sugar in your body and if you are hypertensive, it dilutes the salt in the body and flushes it out), improves constipation, improves headaches, migraines and mood, and protects our joints and keeps them lubricated. On a side note, water also takes care of hangovers. The biggest advantage of drinking water when it comes to weight loss is that when the body is hungry, it is unable to differentiate between dehydration and hunger; therefore, drinking a glass of water can steer one away from any unhealthy cravings.

The ideal amount of water to drink per day varies from body to body. On an average, eight glasses of water should be had daily in the form of plain water, soup, herbal tea or milk. I usually tell my patients to drink water depending on the colour of their urine. If the colour is yellow, they need to have an additional glass of water. Let your urine colour guide you throughout the day.

Lack of water consumption causes dehydration, kidney stones, digestive issues, fatigue, headaches and mood swings.

What kind of water should you be drinking?

Avoid drinking from plastic bottles. Make sure the water is safe and well boiled before you drink it, as water can carry a lot of germs.

Depending on the source, water can be alkaline or slightly acidic. Spring water is usually more alkaline than tap water. However, if you want to have a water alkalising machine, it is totally up to you, because they tend to be very expensive.

RO water: Purifying water via reverse osmosis (RO) is one of the easiest available techniques for an average person. RO basically means that the water flows through a semi-permeable membrane and carbon filters, leaving behind impurities and chemicals. RO water is safe for drinking but can be low in minerals compared to spring water. If you are cooking with RO water, you may lose more vitamins and minerals from the food. However, it is better to consume RO water than ingest harmful chemicals like lead and arsenic. Eventually, how you want to purify or clean your water is your decision.

6. Goodbye, processed food

Processed foods are foods that have undergone a change in their nutrient value from farm to table. They are loaded with preservatives, emulsifiers etc. for longer shelf life.

In earlier times, food was fried to increase its shelf life. These days, we have refrigerators but we still eat fried food, forgetting about trans fats. As I had mentioned earlier, oil, once heated, converts to trans fats—even if it is olive oil.

A packet of chips costs just a few rupees and you can see hundreds of such packets hanging at every corner shop. If you are going to buy and eat them, try to imagine all the trans fats and preservatives that will go into your body. Similarly, if you eat fast food, you have to keep in mind the hidden calories of salt and sugar and low quality fat that may have been used. It is cheap food for a reason.

Our ancestors ate raw, unprocessed food. That is not possible for us in this modern world, but we can try to eat food that is grown locally, bought from farmer's markets, local vegetable vendors, etc.

As I mentioned earlier, try to have the local, staple food that is best suited to your climate. A south Indian will thrive on rice in south India, but perhaps not so much in north India. There are many patients of mine who I try to put on the local food diet. They do well because of the availability of the food and the climate of the place.

You might even consider growing your own herbs and green leafy vegetables. They can be grown in large pots, in case you have space issues.

Today, pesticides are used heavily to increase production. This has been making our bodies inflamed, contributing to various diseases and obesity. Growing organic or sourcing organic food is not a fad—it really helps. Organic farmers use natural manure as fertilizer. You can also purchase compost or make your own for your kitchen garden. Buying organic food might seem heavy on the pocket right now, but in the long run, you will actually reduce the cost of the doctor's fees as well as medication by eating good quality food.

Eating home-cooked foods is another important thing.

Going to a restaurant that serves healthy food is another option.

7. Getting the most out of the local vegetable vendor

Do you know that our local vegetable vendor carries about fifty different types of vegetables and fruits? Yet, when it comes to being creative in the kitchen, we still make the same aloo gobhi or bhindi or beans aloo. The majority of people do not look past just a few staple vegetables or fruits. All you need is to experiment with new vegetables and try them to discover their benefits. For instance, broccoli is extremely anti-cancerous and elephant foot yam is very good for post-menopausal women. I suggest you buy new vegetables every day, or try a new vegetable at least once every week. Start with greens and then explore as many colours as possible. The more colourful the plate, the greater the nutritive value. In terms of fruits, choose them smartly: pick fruits that are low in the glycaemic index and are dark-coloured. Most fruits are rich in fibre and vitamins, but remember that they can be rich in sugars as well, so it is best not to overdo fruits either. Having just a bowl of fruits for a meal is not a great idea; a meal should comprise of all food groups. Of course, fruits are certainly beneficial for a sugar fix in case you have a craving for sweets. So, instead of having chocolate chip cookies, grab a banana.

> *A list of common fruits, from the sweetest to the minimally sweet (in descending order of fructose content):*
>
> Banana
> Chiku (Sapodilla)
> Shahtoot (Mulberry)
> Grapes
> Ripe papaya
> Custard apple
> Watermelon
> Muskmelon
> Soft pear
> Apple
> Green apple
> Pineapple
> Orange
> Hard pear
> Grapefruit
> Ber (wild berries)
> Guava
> Strawberry
> Blueberry

8. Reading food labels

In most households in India, my clients send their staff to shop, or shop online—which is not advisable as you are unable to read the nutrition labels. There are many who do shop themselves, however. For them, reading labels is very helpful for maintaining health or reducing weight.

Being a smart shopper is important and it is important to get a basic idea of how to read a label.

Reading labels of basic food items like rice, flour and oils is hardly useful as they are bought in bulk. On the other hand, labels for snacks-on-the-go, kids' snacks and so-called healthy snacks should be carefully skimmed for the real ingredients.

a. First of all, you must read the serving size and how many calories each serving size contains. Any packet of food can contain more than one serving size. And calories are mentioned as per 100 gm mostly—serving size is less than half of that.

b. Then read the calories, which are sometimes not based on serving sizes but on the whole packet. You can divide the calories as per the serving sizes mentioned.

c. Most importantly, check the carbohydrates, which make up the maximum weight of the snack. Carbohydrates convert to sugar to provide energy; they consist of fibre and sugar. The more fibre a food has, the less its sugar content. Let me make it easier to remember—avoid anything that has sugar more than 20 per cent or fibre less than 5 per cent. If you are aiming to drop kilos, then drop most snacks immediately.

Sometimes, sugar is present in milk, honey, dates, figs etc.; they are mostly harmless but you must consider where you are healthwise. For diabetics, every molecule of sugar or carbohydrate counts. 'Sugar free' products have some form of added artificial sugar. Often these products cause bloating or memory loss when used over a long period of time. Some products are sugar free and some have no added sugar. Know the difference. Corn syrup, fructose, sucrose, concentrated juices, dextrose, maltose are all terms used for added sugar on labels. You must limit their use.

Let me note here that sugar is a natural flavour. To have more or less of it is a taster's choice—you can tune yourself either way slowly.

d. Now for fat calories: You must check the calories that come from fat out of the total calories on the label. Let's say that there are 250 calories in total, and calories from fat are 120. That is almost half and therefore, it is a very calorie-dense food.

There are a lot of types of fat mentioned: saturated, trans fats, cholesterol etc. You must limit the use of saturated fats, especially if you live a sedentary lifestyle. Trans fats should always be zero on the label. Cholesterol should not be more than 300 mg per day in a recommended 2000 calorie diet. If there are terms like monosaturated or polyunsaturated fats mentioned, then just look for low single digit values.

e. Proteins: Let me make this clear—if a person is above 4 years old, there is no protein limit set. Medically, the limit is decided on a case-to-case basis and balancing the meals is the best course of action.

Proteins are essential for energy, hair, nails,

hormone synthesis and immunity. Protein-rich snacks should be preferred over less or no protein snacks. Foods containing protein break down slowly in the stomach; they are much more satisfying and make you less hungry. If you see the example label given below, it contains protein of 5.4 gm per 35 gm, which is a good amount.

f.   Sodium: You must reduce the sodium consumption (sodium chloride or table salt) in your diet. If you have packaged foods, you may find lots of sodium in them. You must note that the recommended daily allowance is not more than half a teaspoon—that is, 1500 mg in the whole day. I have seen that many packets in India don't mention the sodium content, so you must be careful and look for other markers.

g.   Percent daily values: The DV percentage is the daily value recommendation for key nutrients for a 2000 calorie diet (values need to be adjusted as per body weight). Many labels will mention this at the bottom. Reading labels is an art that gets better with time. Lesser percentage is almost always better, except for protein.

Nutritional Information

Nutrients	Per 100 gm#	Per 35 gm#
Energy Value	399 kcal	140 kcal
Protein	15.3 gm	5.4 gm
Carbohydrate	65.8 gm	23.0 gm
Sugar	0 gm	0 gm

Dietary Fibre	15.8 gm	5.5 gm
Soluble Dietary Fibre	4.9 gm	1.7 gm
Insoluble Dietary Fibre	10.9 gm	3.8 gm
Fat	8.3 gm	2.9 gm
Saturated Fatty Acids	1.3 gm	0.5 gm
Monounsaturated Fatty Acids	3.9 gm	1.4 gm
Polyunsaturated Fatty Acids	2.9 gm	1.0 gm
Trans Fatty Acids	0 gm	0 gm
Cholesterol	0 mg	0 mg
Iron	5.4 mg	1.9 mg

#Approximate values   Serving size = 35 gm
Recommended: 2 serving per day
*As per Codex Alimentarius Commission Guidelines

Apart from reading labels, in order to maintain good health or lose weight or prevent ageing, it is very important to shop for the food that matches your criteria. We all want to keep our families healthy and not go over the budget. So, here is what you need to avoid. Most packaged foods are a no-no, but that doesn't mean that you should end up buying nothing. Go for vegetables and fruits first, and then depend on packaged foods for the remaining part of your shopping. Most people buy cereals, pulses and snacks in packets. Pulses and some whole grain cereals are fine, but snacks with a long shelf life have to be bought smartly using the label reading techniques explained above. Instant cereals consumed too often can contribute to unnecessary weight gain. Make your own oatmeal if you can.

Buying nuts in packets is fine, but clean them well at home before use if they come unpackaged. Well packed nuts are well cleaned and sealed. Go for such packets as you can seal them and eat them whenever you like.

Organic foods are very popular these days. There is no way to prove whether they are truly organic and therefore, you must choose a good, known brand. There are good brands available; you only have to do some research. Organic vegetables look natural, are aromatic and have a very low shelf life. There are some legit organic vegetable growers whom you can find online. They don't cost a whole lot more, so that mental block should be removed.

Are you confused about buying frozen foods? You can buy frozen cut vegetables, meats and fish in raw condition. Anything with added sauces—or frozen after being breaded or fried—is absolutely not recommended. Make chicken nuggets at home. Buy fresh pizza or make it at home with good quality cheese and homemade sauce. Most raw meat, fish and vegetables don't lose nutrients on being frozen. Frozen food can be very handy if you have no time to go grocery shopping.

Buying sugar and sugar substitutes:

Say no to white sugar. A good choice is palm sugar, but that can be too expensive sometimes. Therefore, you can try unprocessed sugar or pure maple syrup or real organic honey. Go for organic honey from a good brand. Use sugary stuff sparingly in any case, even if it is pure in quality.

Sugar substitutes are in abundance and so much

confusion has risen so as to what choice to make. Go for the herbal ones like stevia (derived from plant called *Stevia Rebudiana*) which are not absorbed by the body—they are excreted.

Don't fall prey to ordering food from outside too frequently, as there will definitely be some hidden sodium, sugars and badly reused oil.

9. Tips and quick fixes

i. Controlling overeating

Overeating, sometimes, is a mind game and sometimes, it is just hormones wreaking havoc in your body. Sometimes greed takes over hunger and sometimes, low sugar and high ghrelin make you hungry. Some people are compulsive munchers and they end up gaining a lot of weight. The question is, can we train our minds against eating constantly or eating more than we need to?

Sometimes, we can train our minds with careful eating behaviour. Always sit down to eat, and do not rush during mealtimes. Eat slowly and chew each bite at least forty times to make the mind realize that the stomach has been fed. That way, one can avoid both bloating and the desire to eat again shortly. Your sense of fulfilment will also be much higher. Organizing your meals by predetermined timings can also prevent you from overeating. If you are not well fed, you may have the urge to eat whatever comes your way—as hunger is a natural phenomenon of the body. Make sure the body is actually hungry and not just thirsty. Sometimes, our bodies cannot differentiate between hunger and thirst. The hormone ghrelin, as I have mentioned above, is a hunger hormone. When its levels are high, we feel hungry. Therefore, to keep it under control, eating timely is the best way, and also to avoid overeating.

ii. Controlling snacking in between meals/post-dinner snacking

Staying well hydrated is the easiest way to control eating in between meals. Eating a small healthy snack is another good way to avoid large portions. Snacking is not bad if done in really controlled portions; otherwise you will end up eating almost a whole meal in between, on top of having four or five meals a day. Post-dinner snacking can be avoided by eating a well-balanced dinner. Sometimes, you just want a change in taste, so you can have fennel seeds or unflavoured betel nut or cardamom post dinner.

iii. Beating the junk food habit

Junk foods are truly a bad habit, but sometimes due to additives—especially the agents used for flavouring or enhancing taste like monosodium glutamate (MSG)—they are very addictive. I hear so often from patients that they crave certain foods. Most of the time, it is the lack of some micronutrient in your body that is making you crave something with lots of sugar or salt. Craving for junk food can also be a result of starving yourself or giving up on some macronutrient completely. Now your body is trying to compensate for that loss by giving you unhealthy salt or sugar cravings.

iv. Cut back on the sugar

Sugar is the most addictive substance—even more than cocaine. As per some studies, sugar causes overstimulation of the reward areas in the brain. Sugar is present in all carbohydrates—and while some amount of that may be necessary for the body, consuming sugar in itself is not necessary. Massive sugar intake can lead to diabetes, obesity, heart disease, cancer and decreased longevity. Just like alcohol, sugar intake also develops tolerance— which means that you need more to get the same pleasure that you did when you started eating it. Sugar or sugar-laden foods are the easiest to get when cravings set in. All sugar is eventually converted to fat, much more than starch. Excess sugar consumption leads to depression, low self-esteem, migraines, allergies, asthma, risk of antisocial behaviour (even in children) etc.

v. The secrets of salt

Salt is made up of 40 per cent sodium and 60 per cent chloride. As per the American Heart Association and the American Diabetes Association, a person should consume less than 1500-2300 mg of salt per day—approximately a teaspoon a day. No one can survive without sodium, as it is a crucial electrolyte for the body. Sodium maintains an intracellular and extracellular fluid balance. When people talk about water retention with increased sodium intake, it is because sodium tends to bind with water, thus mildly increasing blood pressure.

Having said that, consuming sodium from homemade food and from packaged processed food are two entirely different things. Packaged food and snacks are laden with high quantities of sodium—sometimes more than double the normal value that we need. A lot of hidden salt is present in commercially prepared food and in takeouts, especially in Chinese food and Mughlai food.

When we talk about lowering salt content in the diet, it primarily means giving up on junk and processed foods. A lot of doctors and nutritionists will tell patients to reduce salt intake for weight loss, even though there isn't much evidence to support that claim. People eating very little salt end up having low blood pressure; some can even develop hypothyroidism due to their restricted intake of salt, which is the only iodized food product available to man.

The DASH (Dietary Approach to Stop Hypertension) diet is recommended for prevention and reduction of hypertension and risk of heart disease. It promotes fruits, vegetables and lean proteins.

The harmful effects caused by decreasing salt intake include insulin resistance and hyponatremia in athletes and risk of hypothyroidism due to lack of iodine in general. Salt deficiencies can manifest as weakness, headache, fatigue, muscle cramps, vomiting and confusion.

Many studies have shown that sodium follows a J-shaped curve, which means that it is harmful if too much or too little is taken. Sometimes people end up consuming more salt if they are on low carb diets.

A word about Himalayan pink salt, also known as sendha namak or rock salt:

Himalayan pink salt is an unprocessed form of salt; it is superior to table salt as the latter can contain anti-clumping agents which are actually chemicals that harm health. Therefore, using rock salt or Himalayan pink salt is a better choice than using white salt. Himalayan pink salt mostly comes from the region of Punjab and contains about eighty-four minerals and trace elements. Rock salt contains a compound of magnesium which helps in sleep improvement as well. But overdoing rock salt, again, has its downsides. I believe that taste alteration takes time— whether it is sweets or salt, whether it is potassium, sodium or magnesium. Lowering the craving for such tastes happens slowly as it takes time for the taste buds to change.

We all need a break at times and here is my ultimate cheat food diet plan:

Breakfast: Some form of protein shake OR plain yoghurt with nuts and a piece of fruit

Mid-morning: Coconut water OR buttermilk OR lemon water with salt

Lunch: Chicken or vegetable salad with oil dressing (no sugary dressing) OR protein only, like chicken or paneer (about palm size serving)

Evening: Tea with no sugar and five to eight almonds

Dinner: Vegetable/chicken soup OR Chinese food/ Japanese food (order mostly vegetables and proteins)/ sushi/Thai curry and steamed rice

Low-calorie drinks: Only alcoholic drinks which are low in calorie content are to be had (that too, only in moderation), like vodka water, tequila water, Bacardi water, a glass of wine, champagne or Bloody Mary

In non-alcoholic drinks: salty lemonade or lemon soda, diluted fruit juices with lots of ice and mint, virgin mojito with sugar substitute, diet soda (not my favourite but can be had occasionally if you don't drink alcohol), pure coconut water (not from a bottled source), tomato juice

A healthy eating-out guide can easily consist of options from various cuisines like Chinese, Mughlai, Continental and Indian.

Chinese: Steamed rice/rice noodles and vegetables like mushrooms and bokchoy in black bean sauce

Mughlai: Nihari, paaya, galouti kebab, keema, mutton kebabs (since they are all roasted/grilled). Fried food and thick creamy gravies should be avoided. Have tandoori roti instead of naan and plain curd instead of boondi raita. Cut back portions of biryani, eat from a small plate, opt for little or no desserts (and share if you have them) and chew a lot.

Continental: There are lots of options in this cuisine. Salads without sugary dressings, grilled chicken, steak, grilled vegetables, many non-fried egg dishes like devilled eggs, whole wheat pasta salad, pasta in pesto (not white) creamy sauce, cheese and crackers, vegetable wraps, stuffed tomatoes or peppers, any vegetarian or non-vegetarian skewers, fruit salads without cream

Chapter 4

Food Myths

Weight loss is, as we all know, not an easy process. These days, there is an overload of information on 'healthy food' and 'weight loss tips' that promise to give you results. Many kinds of weight loss advice are doled out on social media, websites and other unreliable mediums. These food myths are often treated like the gospel truth. Following such food and weight loss advice may harm your health rather than help in the long run, and also make you actually gain weight rather than lose it!

One such recent trend is that of people following a fad diet. An important thing to remember is that a person on a fad diet will almost certainly relapse into binge eating behaviour. Therefore, they have to make changes in their lifestyle—small changes, one at a time. When we try to follow any such diet (the word 'dieting' is itself a deterrent to diets, as it is a long-term lifestyle change), we give up on the nutrients of a balanced meal plan. Therefore, the body becomes deficient in essential nutrients, which upsets its harmony—and that is something which will lead to hunger pangs or binge eating or cravings for a certain food type. Try not to follow these fads. They will leave your body starving and stressed out with increased or decreased cortisol, leading to fat deposition around the waist or upper body. I have seen people going on diets consisting of only proteins, or only fruits, or only single grains or legumes, fatless diets, or diets with too much fat. As I explained, these will leave your body craving for other nutrients as well as making it resistant to weight loss when taken too far. Sometimes, doctors have to use very low calorie diets, but that is only recommended under strict supervision. Otherwise, a well-balanced diet is the way to go.

1. Fad diets

Fruit diet:

When we eat too much fruit, we increase the level of potassium in our body and therefore end up losing more water in the form of urine.

If we only eat fruits the entire day, we are cutting back on salt and therefore not eating the right nutrients—because there is no fat, no other minerals and no protein. Some people even drink fruit juices on such diets and they do this for a prolonged period.

The downside to this diet is that you break down muscle, binge eat after the diet is over, grow deficient in sodium—due to which there is muscle weakness—and increase insulin levels due to high consumption of sugar, thus making it a risk factor for insulin resistance.

Liquid diets:

In such diets, people end up drinking only juices, teas, soups and, again, restrict salt and chewing. For example, we have the cabbage soup diet, which is followed by a lot of people and has gained a lot of momentum over the last few years. If such a diet is done properly under supervision using protein supplements, then it can be of benefit, but again it is not a long-term plan.

The downside is muscle breakdown, lack of nutrients, poor overall maintenance and vengeful eating. There is also a risk of formation of kidney stones and gall stones.

Low fat/low carb diet:

This is one of the worst forms of diet, especially for young people. If you cut down fat from your diet, you basically end up not synthesizing the good hormones and lose hair, get bad skin, bad nails and bone problems. Since most of the fat soluble vitamins like Vitamins A, D, E and K are not absorbed in the body, you end up getting all the side effects of this neglect, such as nerve problems, hormonal issues and other problems mentioned above. A few other side effects include kidney/gall stones, low fertility, low libido and constipation.

Extremely low calorie diets:

In these diets, people eat upto 500-600 calories a day. Unless done under medical supervision, this kind of diet will make you dehydrated, fatigued, nauseous and dizzy as your body is set to function at a certain calorie need.

You can also get gall stones, kidney stones, constipation, fissures and piles.

High protein diets:

In this diet, proteins are usually eaten in the form of animal proteins, which most people tend to overeat. People also tend to eat processed meats. If not done under medical supervision, these diets can cause osteoporosis, kidney stones, gall stones, constipation, piles and vitamin deficiencies.

All these above-mentioned plans are called different names on different websites. As a patient, you should first seek consultation from a healthcare professional about what plan you should follow. If the above plans are followed properly, they can benefit some people, but if you blindly trust the internet or untrained friends—it's a terrible idea.

Let us bust some myths about fad diets and weight loss:

1. *I can do a juice fast and lose 10 kilos.*
   NO, you can't. It's only water loss that shows up on the scale. Liquid diets such as those with juices only cause water loss and muscle loss. When you start eating again you will put on weight again, and probably gain even more.
2. *I can lose weight by eating a lot and exercising a lot.*
   NO. Eighty per cent of a diet is lifestyle changes that you will have to make.
3. *I can have dals as my proteins and lose weight.*

NO. Dals also have carbs, so they are great—but you need other kinds of protein too.

4. *I can get liposuction for weight/fat loss.*
   NO. Liposuction is designed for people with near normal BMI.

5. *I always lose weight when I diet, so I can do it. I just don't find time.*
   NO. Whatever weight loss you managed was wrong, because you put the weight back on.

6. *I can starve and lose weight.*
   NO. You are lowering your basal metabolic rate and when you eat, your fat cells will double in size again.

7. *I want to just lose fat on my belly.*
   There's no way you can do that without an exercise and diet routine.

8. *I eat very healthy but I still don't lose weight.*
   NO, you are probably eating something during the day that piles up fat in your body without you being aware of it.

9. *I eat only salads and vegetables and I manage to lose weight, but the fat comes back in some months.*
   Yes, you can lose weight that way, but if you haven't added protein, you are losing muscle proteins and the weight loss will not last.

10. *I can't find time, life is so busy.*
    NO. You can find time to eat/sleep/make money. Why not keep an hour for yourself? Trust me; it is the best investment you can make with your time.

A fad dieter is the kind of patient who is always looking for quick solutions for weight loss. They think that with such a fad diet, they will be able to lose all their excess weight in a month or so. As I already explained, weight gain does not happen in such a short period of time; so, why expect to lose weight like that?

I have a number of such patients. When my brother, Randeep, was made to lose a lot of weight for his film *Sarbjit*, I had numerous people pouring in asking for quick solutions. As I explained to everyone then and will do again now—he is a film star, he had a goal in mind and that was his motivation. He wanted to get into a character. But most of us live in the real world, where we have many other things to do instead of working day in and day out to suit ourselves to a role. Randeep had calorie restrictions, as well as frequent blood testing and EKGs to make sure that there were no deleterious effects on his health.

I was monitoring him day and night—he had given up his social life. I didn't want to do this in the first place because I was against him losing this much weight, but he was adamant. He convinced me that there was no one better than me who knew him and his health. I took up the task reluctantly but was determined that he would keep up his health and well-being. When drastic weight loss happens, muscle loss is very high and it takes time to rebuild that lost muscle. So unless medically indicated, very low calorie diets are reserved for heavily obese patients under strict supervision.

Case study of a fad dieter

Let me tell you about this particular patient who came in looking for an express weight loss solution. She had followed many fad short term diets in the past. Any fad diet—you name it, she had done it. She was always successful in losing weight in the short term, but it always came back—and even more was added.

So here she was, looking slightly depressed, anxious to start the weight loss programme:

Age: 43

Sex: F

Weight: 87.9 kg

BMI: 33

Max weight till date: 87.9 kg

Min weight in the last five years: 64 kg

Previous medical issues: Removal of gall bladder, liposuction, depression, PCOS, PHQ screening score for depression is 15, which is very high.

Exercise status: Rare

Diet recall:

Breakfast: Toast or eggs, or uttapam, or poha and fruit

Lunch: Roti and dahi, dal and vegetables

Evening snack: Tea and cookies

Dinner: Variable, could be chinese, or continental, or simple roti and sabzi

Social history: Rarely drinks alcohol and smokes six cigarettes per day

Sleep: 6-7 hours

Water intake: Not much

Supplements: None

Medications: PCOS medications but not regularly, vitamins on and off

Plan: Her depression screening score was a red flag for me instantly. She was referred to a psychiatrist who she followed up with in a couple days; she had a history of depression and needed professional help. Coming to her plan—she, as usual, wanted weight loss as quickly as possible. She often felt hungry and would eat late at night daily.

She had tried numerous diets on her own—even went for a liposuction—and still put all the weight right back on. If liposuction was a viable alternative to a lifestyle change, I would ask everyone to go for it. However, it is not and therefore, you must change your lifestyle for good. Following fads, losing weight and then putting it right back is not a healthy, well-balanced lifestyle. Liposuction can be a good solution for the stubborn fat that remains after you have tried to change your lifestyle by eating healthy and exercising.

Alongside being depressed about her weight, she was also not an active person. She would rarely exercise and that bothered me. If not for weight loss, you must still exercise for endorphins, the happy hormones. After checking her blood work, which was normal, I had just the plan for her.

I started her off on a ketogenic diet plan, which includes proteins and fats but no starch, for a short duration. People find this on the Internet, but the ketogenic plan is not for everyone. Here we have someone who doesn't care about what she eats as long as her stomach is full; she doesn't know how to react to hunger cravings, or have any idea that a healthy snack is so much better than calorie dense foods even if they seem smaller.

The patient was very compliant and I had no problems giving her weekly plans. By the end of week one, she had lost 3 kg, and felt great and motivated. I checked the ketones in her urine—she was following her diet religiously.

The next step was to add good quality carbohydrates. She shortlisted what she could and couldn't eat.

She kept pushing me to do more of a protein and fat combination, but I knew that was not going to be too fruitful as it was going to become just another fad for her. She needed to learn—so I gave her a huge shopping list and asked her to go look for the stuff I was recommending, the names of some of which she hadn't even heard.

She made weekly visits, and during each visit, I would discuss the importance of eating whole foods for the rest of her life. She had to eat proper satisfactory meals.

She had lost 5.5 kg by the end of three weeks and was still going strong. Now she is on both high and low calorie diets, on alternate days, because of which she will stick to the plan. She feels a lot better too. She regularly visits her psychiatrist and has restarted her medications. She has started exercising slowly, as per her comfort, although she does not go to the gym yet. Now she needs to learn how to control her hunger.

With our combined efforts, I am sure she will come out a winner.

2. Weight loss myths

i. Skipping meals: Many people think that starving or over-exercising is the easiest way to lose weight. Some even think that popping a supplement or a fat burner will help, while others have told me that when they skip meals, they lose weight—or when they follow a certain diet, eating the same food for the whole day, they lose weight. The most ridiculous myth I have come across is the idea that eating only low fat or fat-free foods is the most effective for weight-loss.

ii. Having low fat foods: People have stopped eating egg yolk because of all the incorrect information available to us through magazines and other forms of media. Avoiding ghee and nuts has also become rampant. No one accounts for the benefits of good fats. Fats don't make you fat; sugar, in fact, is what leads to fat deposit. We have ignored fats and their goodness for the longest time, making fat the enemy. Cholesterol is responsible for many important physiological processes in our body. Fats are useful for hormone synthesis and cell membrane synthesis; they insulate us, protect our vital organs and help absorb nutrients from our food. All the fat soluble vitamins like A,

D, E and K are only absorbed if you consume enough fat in your diet. Fat makes you full, lowering your appetite. For all these reasons, moderate consumption of fat is actually a good thing.

iii. Mono diet concept: Mono diets seem to work for some people and not for others. I like to label it as a fad diet because, after all, having the same food for all three meals almost never works. If it does, it's because you're compensating for past eating or future eating habits. These kinds of diet regimes encourage binge eating behaviour. There is absolutely no scientific evidence to support such diets and they were probably created to fulfil some kind of fad. Even if they do help you drop some pounds, it is because you are probably losing water weight and burning fat. Water shifts are huge when you change your diet, and if you understand that, you will never fall for such atrocities.

iv. Liquid diets: A very low calorie diet (VLCD) is the toughest of all diets. It involves eating about 800 calories a day. Unless done under medical supervision, these VLCD diets can be very dangerous. Doctors might prescribe these kinds of diets at times before a surgery, when they need rapid weight loss. But it is done carefully, with the right macronutrients in place and making sure that all the lab work is done before starting the diet regimen, while on the regimen, and after the plan is completed. This kind of diet doesn't mean having juices to fill ourselves up—it means that we make sure that muscle breakdown doesn't happen while trying to lose weight. Once muscle breakdown happens, people gain weight very soon after the completion of the diet and the weight gain usually doubles, if not done carefully. You must contact a physician or a registered dietician before you think of going on such diets.

3. Myths surrounding health foods

Fat free vs sugar free

Most of us will fall for phrases such as 'diet food' or 'fat free food'. What does it mean to have these foods? What should be the quantity and portion sizes? Why do they matter? What's the logic behind it? Here is a breakdown of some diet or fat free foods and why you should have or avoid them.

i. Grains and biscuits: Oats biscuits are laden with sugar, and have refined flour too. Therefore, you must read the labels before buying them. The carbohydrate content decreases when the fibre content goes up. Brown breads are not always whole grains and are mixed with sugar and refined flour. Sometimes even colour is added to it to make it brown. Multigrain biscuits (cookies) are the same as oats cookies, laden with sugar and bleached flour. Sometimes, they even have grain remnants from the mill, which are of extremely bad quality. Brown rice has a lower glycemic index and if you're considering eating it in large quantities believing it to be healthy, you must know that it has as many calories as white rice. The only difference is the slightly higher fibre content.

ii. Diet snacks: Diet snacks are packed with sugar or bad fats/oil. They might be roasted, but do not buy them if they are improperly labelled. Most diet snacks are eaten in large quantities by people who think they can eat that much since they are diet snacks. The rule is to have snacks in small quantities, even if it seems low in calories.

iii. Fat free or skimmed foods: These foods are labelled as skimmed or fat free but did you know that the *moment we remove fat from milk, the sugar content goes up?* In a lot of fat free products, you will find the sugar is high as they have to flavour it if it is fat free. Take bottled salad dressings, for instance. They are labelled fat free and have loads of sugar and we feel that we are having a salad and still piling pounds as the sugar is not going to let us lose weight.

iv. Flavoured Greek yoghurt: This kind of yoghurt, which is higher in protein, is enriched with sugar. Therefore, it is best to avoid it. Buy a plain one instead and add fruits to it to make it tastier.

v. Bhelpuri: A lot of people think that bhelpuri is a healthy snack, but it has a lot of sugar due to the sauces used. The ingredients are fried, causing inflammation to the body which might lead to weight gain.

vi. Momos (dimsums): Steamed dimsums are better than fried ones, yes. However, the problem is that the maida coating on the dimsum is a high glycemic index food. It is a refined flour and consuming it will raise your insulin.

vii. Too many fruits: Fruits are healthy for the body but consuming too many fruits is again a problem. Fruits also contain sugar. It may be natural, but sugar is sugar. Having fruits in the evening will make them ferment in the belly, causing bloating and uneasiness. Therefore, I recommend not having too many fruits and keeping it balanced in your diet.

viii. Milk: Milk is for children, but so much milk is consumed by adults. The process of milk extraction is not a pleasant one, as you might know if you have seen professional milk extraction machines. It is painful to see how cows have their udders pinned to a machine. I discourage the consumption of milk. It is not the only source of protein for vegetarians. Read the protein section and take your pick, and give up milk completely if possible.

ix. White butter or ghee or coconut oil: They are better fats but in large quantities, they too will help you pick up pounds. Fat is a dense calorie, so unless you are advised by your physician to eat a lot of it, be careful about how much you consume.

x. Murmure (rice flakes): They may seem light—that's why lots of people eat them. They forget that murmure is white rice, and causes insulin to increase and store the fat.

xi. Frying in olive oil: Frying is oxidation of fat and if you repeatedly use the same oil or ghee for frying, you have oxidized the fat so much that when you consume the food, you will only be eating toxins. It causes inflammation in the body, leading to obesity and numerous other issues.

xii. Dips and cracker combo: A lot of people love chips with dips. If you think this is one of the healthiest things to eat, then you are mistaken. The dip may already be heavy in fat, but as soon as you combine it with a carbohydrate (the crackers), then you are in for some serious weight gain. Try to have dips with fruits or vegetables like cucumbers, peppers, celery, apple slices, carrots etc.

Case study of a patient on a constant diet plan/always trying to lose weight

I think this variety of patients tops my list. I have so many of them that to narrow them down to one example was very tough. However, I picked the one who came frequently enough to leave a lasting impression on my mind. She was 45 years old and has been on one or the other diet for the last twenty years.

She was a marathon runner and complained of weight gain for the last one year, even after trying to lose weight on her own. She had hypothyroidism, which was well controlled. She was peri menopausal (nearing menopause) and her periods had started wreaking havoc; hot flashes had set in, and she was gaining weight on her arms. She exercised a lot and had always been a runner. Her lean muscle mass was not quite good and her fat percentage was also quite high as per her exercise routine. So I ran a few tests and noted all her statistics.

Age: 45

Sex: F

Weight: 65 kg

BMI: 26.2

Max weight till date: 72 kg

Min weight in last five years: 60 kg

Medical illnesses: Hypothyroidism, irregular periods, bloating, sweet cravings

Exercise status: Runs marathons

Diet recall: Vegetarian, rarely eats eggs and generally eats poha, upma, roti, sabzi, the usual north Indian food, but in exceeding portions.

Sleep: 6 hours

Water intake: Consciously drinks water

Supplements: None

Medications: For hypothyroid

Plan: If I see anyone with bloating and sweet cravings, the first thing I do is stop the probable foods causing it. For her, bread and anything with yeast was stopped immediately. I laid stress on practicing chewing every bite for at least thirty times. All refined flour was out, all milk was stopped and I only kept cottage cheese and yoghurt. She had to give up all sugar at once. I don't taper sugar if someone has bloating. Sugar consumption generates sugar craving.

She exercised hard even though I was not in favour of that. Many articles suggest that people with sluggish thyroid should do less strenuous workouts. Also, in my experience, hypothyroid patients should not be sedentary but should not exercise too much either—it is harmful either way for them.

I increased her protein and fat intake for two weeks, which scared her a lot, and gave her lots of vegetables with yoghurt for lunch. She could have nuts in the next phase. She had to hold back the consumption of yoghurt, too, for the first few days.

Two weeks later, she dropped 3 kg and then I started her on alternate flour (barring wheat) roti for lunch. Jowar was my first preference, but one can choose any of the options between quinoa, soya, chickpea etc. I kept her protein intake high because of how physically active she was.

In just a month, her bloating had disappeared. That's when I added well-cooked lentils for lunch. She liked her dals so I re-introduced that. Some bloating reappeared with lentils, which was not bad overall because most whole lentils are prebiotics—which means they work in your gut to improve its lining.

Over a period of time, she achieved decent weight loss and improvement in her lean muscle mass. She also ran less and started mild weightlifting. As we age, muscles hypotrophy as a result of less use. One has to start adding resistance to make sure the tone is maintained. She is now taking protein supplements to complete her protein requirements, along with egg on particular days. Her main area of focus was her arms and for that, she must get her weight uniformly down. It is a myth that you can reduce weight from a part of your body; weight loss affects all areas, although for some it is more hard work than others.

She did not eat junk food anyway, so I didn't have to work on that. Her sweet cravings still happened sometimes, especially at night. Therefore, I added some prunes as her bedtime snack. That way she could have her micronutrients, fibre and taste at the same time. She loved them and we are both happy with that.

I still see her once in a while, when she has travelled and has gained some weight. Breads are out of her life; she is focusing on whole foods rather than refined ones. Along with proteins and fat, a small amount of seasonal fruits, some nuts and a whole lot of vegetables have become the mainstays of her diet. She promises to not use the sentence, 'I am on a diet,' but rather tells herself that she eats healthy.

Exercise, too, is not free of myths. We must never overdo anything—and that includes exercise.

Exercise is a part of daily life, but the human body is not designed to exert too much energy in the gym or on machines. Functional fitness, which I shall elaborate on later, is the best form of exercise—but most of us want to achieve some target, such as building muscle, losing fat in particular areas, fitting into specific clothes, or working towards a media-created standard.

For most people, when they want to lose weight or start maintaining a healthy lifestyle, the first thing that comes to their mind is the gym. They end up joining a gym, paying the high subscription fees, and within a few days, get extremely tired and eventually stop going to the gym altogether. Some people work out for many months, but still don't lose weight or achieve their target. This frustrates them because they had thought exercising would change the way they looked. Many people over-exercise and inhibit their growth hormone release, thus upsetting the hormone balance of the body. And so no results are obtained from exercising.

Effective exercise is anything that raises your heart rate above normal. If you're used to walking a certain distance at a certain speed, to get better results, you have to change your intensity or duration. In my experience, I have seen many people using their time to walk 6-7 kms a day, and yet they can't maintain this for a long period of time because they will not always have as much time as they have today. The best form of exercise is to do something you can maintain all your life.

The biggest myth is that exercising is the best way to lose weight. As I mentioned previously, the food you eat accounts for 80 per cent of how you look and how much weight you have; 10-15 per cent is exercise and the remaining 5 per cent we can blame on genetics. In fact, people who start working out a lot get very hungry and have no idea how to control the hunger, because they have not learnt about filling food, or the art of volumetric eating, or the art of having more food and fewer calories. They end up eating condensed forms of calories. So, instead of losing weight, they end up gaining it. To sum it up, changing your eating pattern is more important than heading to the gym.

Another exercise myth is about weight training. Many people, especially women, feel that by doing weight training, they will become bigger or have big muscles, or even end up looking like men. In fact, muscles are the metabolic hub of your body, and women don't have enough testosterone to make big muscles. Instead, they burn fat effectively if weight training is added to their routine.

Yet another very big exercise myth is spot reduction

exercise. No exercise can burn fat in any one isolated area. Fat leaves the body uniformly and you cannot lose fat from one particular place just by doing a certain exercise. Abs are made in the kitchen, not in the gym.

One big myth is that you must go for a walk or exercise in the morning. A lot of people think that if you don't work out in the morning, you won't get enough results. Working out at any time of the day will result in fat loss or an increase in metabolism, resulting in a change in the shape of the body. You can work out in the evenings or at night. The only problem with working out at night is that you may develop insomnia.

Another myth is if you're a gym goer, you can sit or lie down the whole day, since you have already burned calories. If you just lie around all day not moving after going to the gym, it will negate the effects of burning calories in the gym. You have to be active throughout the day. Sitting down for a long stretch of time is harmful to your body. In fact, it is now said that sitting is the new smoking.

One of the biggest myths is that having six pack abs is a sign of fitness. Even if you don't have six pack abs, you can still be fit. You should, instead, aim for strength, stamina, and less fatigue to be mentally and physically active. That is the true definition of fitness. Drinking sports drinks after workout is also a harmful practice. A lot of people end up drinking a lot of sugar in the form of sports drinks after their workout sessions and they actually pile on the pounds instead of losing weight. This is because they have more drinks than the energy they burn during their exercise period.

Another false practice is relying too much on cardio machines and wrist gadgets to count calories. They are often inaccurate and might confuse you. The only recourse is to work out enough, comfortably, frequently and persistently and keep eating a good diet and avoid junk food.

One last word. Don't overdo it, because it can lead to injuries. Muscles don't grow if you don't have recovery periods. Excessive breakdown of muscles can lead to aches and pains and it can negate all the effects of the muscle building that you did in the past.

Chapter 5

The Great Urban Indian Lifestyle and Diet Challenge

In this chapter, I shall discuss the urban Indian lifestyle and the challenges that our diets can pose.

1. Stress and weight gain

Modern lives have become very stressful. Whether it is work stress or domestic stress, it is all a part of life. De-stressing is very important and there are ways to do it. Meditation must be mandatory in our lives. However, a lot of people don't know how to meditate. You can take the help of professionals, but if you are someone like me who lacks the time, you can go on YouTube and click on guided meditation videos. It is really easy; you only have to click on a video according to how much time you can spend and meditate. You must do it for at least five minutes a day. You can do that in your car, or at bed time, or in your free time in between work—just put your headphones on. Breathing techniques have been used by Asians to de-stress for ages. Taking deep breaths with long exhalations at least two to three times a day will make you feel better. Stress is deeply connected to weight gain. When your body is under stress, you increase the levels of cortisol (secreted by adrenal glands) in the blood, which increases fat deposition around the waist by supressing the immune system and increasing blood sugar. That is why it is imperative for you to de-stress.

2. A sedentary lifestyle

Most urban Indian households have drivers, cooks and maids, as a result of which people are sitting more and moving less, when standing in the kitchen itself can burn calories. A majority of people don't really enter the kitchen or do grocery shopping, and now almost everything is available online, too. Due to this, our lives have become very sedentary. We hardly walk around unless we purposely go for a walk to the park. Some people don't even take advantage of the parks near the house. Going to the gym is not necessary if a walk daily can be included in a disciplined manner. Drivers have become more of a necessity of this urban life than a luxury; women go through severe mental stress if the maid is gone or a cook takes a leave or leaves the job. We are not used to doing things ourselves anymore, as a result of which obesity is on a very steep rise in urban India.

3. Indian cooking, challenges and solutions

The main problem areas in Indian cooking are high fat content, fried foods, high carbohydrate and overcooking of vegetables.

Indian food is loved across the world and I am proud of our cuisine. In fact, my friend has even started a healthy Indian food joint in New York. I was impressed to see how little oil they used for cooking, and the fact that they used high protein fillings like shrimps, chicken and cheese in dosas.

Here are my tips for healthy Indian cooking:

1. It is not wrong to educate our mothers, fathers or whoever cooks our food about how to take a healthier approach. The older generation grew up in a different era, when the amount of physical activity was much higher.

2. Begin by standing next to them when they start cooking to let them know that no more than a teaspoon of oil should be used to roast the cumin/ jeera seeds (best is canola/peanut/coconut/ mustard/sesame oil). Don't overheat olive oil. In case you cook yourself, you must follow these instructions too.

3. Use an oil dispenser with a narrow opening while pouring out the oil, as pouring straight from the bottle is very tricky and there is the danger of pouring more than is necessary.

4. Invest in good cookware, use anodized material, and stay away from other non-stick material and aluminum.

5. Don't overcook your vegetables as they lose all their minerals and vitamins. Grill them on the pan or oven. The best thing to do is to use a small

amount of any PUFA (polyunsaturated oils) with a basting brush and brush the oil lightly on the food while it is being cooked.

6. Use a generous amount of haldi (turmeric) as it's known to be healing.

7. Limit halwas, pooris and pakoras for festivities.

8. Roti is very healthy. When you make the dough, make sure that there is fibre in the flour. My personal preference is to add channa flour, wheat bran/oat bran and flaxseed powder. Fibre will decrease the overall carbohydrate in the roti and it's the best fresh bread I have ever eaten. However, more than two rotis will contribute to weight gain.

9. Eat lots of dahi, preferably homemade, which has a lot of probiotic properties and is good for the intestines. In fact, raita (without boondi) and lassi are famous in the USA, available in all health food stores.

10. Do not eat two starchy carbs in the same meal, like rajma (kidney beans) and rice. Switch to brown rice or quinoa.

11. We Indians also tend to eat dessert after supper, and that habit can be curbed by either taking a little walk after dinner or having green tea or chamomile tea.

12. If you are a non-vegetarian, stick to roasted or grilled tandoori foods.

13. In my own experience, many Indian dishes like stuffed baingan (eggplant) or stuffed capsicum

(green pepper) are yummy when baked in the oven.

14. Garnish food with herbs like cilantro (fresh dhaniya). It increases the taste of food and has many antioxidant properties as well as lipid-lowering qualities.

15. Challenge your friends to host the healthiest food parties—especially those who like to do kitty parties.

16. Unless you have high blood pressure, saltless diets are not recommended for weight loss. A recent study shows that low salt consumption can lead to high cholesterol and triglyceride levels and even insulin resistance. Besides, salt is iodized and very important for the functioning of the thyroid glands, especially for people who have sluggish thyroid.

Case study of a patient who wished to conceive

Age: 29

Sex: Female

Weight: 59 kg

BMI: 26

Max weight till date: 70 kg

Min weight in last five years: 40 kg

Previous medical issues: PCOS, infertility, fatty liver, hypothyroid, pre-diabetic

Exercise status: Yoga (previously)

Diet recall: Non-vegetarian

Breakfast: Generally a complex carb with tea or egg and bread

Lunch: Roti with a seasonal vegetable

Snacks: Comprising of seasonal fruits

Dinner: Roti with a seasonal vegetable

Social history: No alcohol or smoking

Sleep: 8-9 hours

Water intake: Sufficient

Supplements: Methylcobal (B12), Vitamin D3 (Uprise), fish oil, Metformin

Medications: Folfil, Doxinale, Zinetac, Susten, Duphastan, Aspisol, Nidoger, Thyronom, Provigil, Toxocare

Plan: In spite of the already acquired health problems, her major concern was that she was unable to conceive. Having tried almost every possible thing, her last option, according to her gynecologist, was IVF (In Vitro Fertilization). Studying her case minutely, I inferred in my experience as a medical practitioner that it would be unfair to give up completely without trying the best medicine, or in other words, food. So, I tried to align her diet in a very balanced way, wherein I could focus on her nutritional needs, and that would take care of her other illnesses as well.

She was a very lethargic person and would get tired even after exercising only a little. I started her on some supplements which included Methylcobal, Vitamin D3, fish oil and Metformin (because she was already a PCOS patient). Her initial diet had comprised of a lot of unhealthy food, so she was strictly asked to cut down on four main things: juices, bread, milk and rice. She was not completely taken off all of them at once, but was made to eliminate them one by one. It would have been very difficult for her to give up on things which she had loved all her life. Nevertheless, she made efforts to make all possible changes in her diet and lifestyle. Unlike most of my other patients, she was very positive and had a strong desire to overcome the situation she was facing.

I started her off with intermittent fasting, which turned out to be a good start. The dosage of her supplements was being changed from time to time, as per the improvement noticed. A significant change which I noticed was her fatigue—one of her major concerns—lessening over time.

After making significant changes in her diet and with the addition of supplements, the next step was to encourage her to incorporate some form of physical activity in her lifestyle. She was prompted to be more active, and also to slowly and gradually increase the intensity of her workouts.

She was doing pretty well with the diet without much complaint. However, in spite of the fact that milk had to be removed from her diet, she insisted on having a cup of tea in the evening—so I agreed to it. Her diet had to be very carefully made because I didn't want to leave any scope for undernourishment. To meet the increasing demand of protein by her body, I advised a protein shake during her diet for a small period of time, very specifically prescribing the exact amount to be taken.

Her breakfast generally composed of a specified

amount of egg whites and yolk or besan/oat bran cheela. The patient was fond of fruits and therefore, was allowed to have a specified amount of low GI fruits for her mid-morning snack, along with a probiotic drink like jeera chaach. A sufficient amount of nuts and seeds were also included as a part of her evening snack so that she could refrain from munching on junk food. Such packaged foods do not get spoiled and therefore, not all packaged foods are malicious. To add some flavour, tulsi/elaichi tea was advised, since she simply could not miss her evening tea. To meet her nutritional needs and to refrain her from having a lot of simple carbohydrates, I advised her to try sweet potato chaat and some fresh coconut on some days, just to add variety in her diet so she wouldn't get bored eating the same foods again and again. Dinners were usually a combination of complex carbs and proteins, so they included paneer or eggs or, sometimes, pulses with bran roti. A cheat meal was allowed on some days, but that too had to be home-cooked. Street food and outside eating were completely barred for her.

During this entire process, I could see her weight dropping significantly, which was crucial in her case, as being overweight can also hinder the process of conception. Although I was pretty positive about her, somewhere down the line of treatment, it was a challenge for me too. I had to align her diet in such a way that her dietary lifestyle would not come in the way of conception.

She kept visiting me regularly for four months. By the end of it, she had lost around 8 kg and that too, in a very healthy way. Thereafter, she was asked to come for a follow-up after six months. But her husband came to see me instead, four months after her last visit.

I was both surprised and sceptical to see him. He came in all smiling and shared what was perhaps his life's biggest news! He told me that his wife was expecting, and the conception had taken place in a natural way and not through IVF—which, if you remember, had initially been suggested to her as the only option left. He was full of gratitude and I was thrilled to bits. A rare case—perhaps a life-changing one for them, and for me as well! I put her on a maintenance plan to make sure all went well during her gestation period. Now she is hale and hearty and of course...glowing!

4. The wedding season

The big fat Indian wedding is an occasion when people tend to really lose control. Weddings in India are generally extended over a period of a few days, as there are many functions. During this time, the person getting married is super stressed while other people are feasting in glory. So, it is these other people I will first talk about. So often a patient will tell me that they have to go to at least four or five weddings in a season, and they will eat all the rich food (which is, of course, yummy) as everyone is focusing on the best cuisines and chefs. The problem is when you end up overindulging. You fall off the graph of your healthy lifestyle. People will invite and you will go, but limiting the food intake, making sure you only choose a couple of food items you would like to have, not going for the entire main course and limiting dessert intake, or eating before going, if you have too many invites—these are the things you must keep in mind.

Now, let me talk about the pre-wedding period of the bride or the groom. I have had many women come to me asking for a way to lose 10-15 kg in a month. One person even had a target of 20 kg in thirty days, without realizing how damaging it is to not just the body, but also the mind. Even the thought of losing so much in such a short span sends shivers down my spine. Everything related to a wedding—the health of your skin, the stress, the mood, the shopping on a hungry stomach, the clothes and measurements etc. can add up to be too much. A wedding is supposed to be a happy time for everyone—why make it so stressful? You must plan ahead of time and have realistic targets. Let me share a general plan with you that most people can follow as preparation before the wedding.

1. Stop all junk and sugar immediately.
2. Get 7-8 hours of sleep.
3. Make a grocery list which comprises of fewer packaged foods and more fresh items like fruits and vegetables and salads.
4. Eat more proteins and less carbs for the preparation time.
5. Incorporate nuts, in a limited amount, in your diet.
6. Stay hydrated at all times.
7. Fast once a week.
8. Exercise if you can, or join a group class for Pilates or yoga.
9. Start meditating, it will come in handy.

10. Limit screen time on phone or TV to avoid dark circles.

5. The last five syndrome

Although many people have their weight in the normal range, they still want to lose more weight. I come across these people who have fluctuating weight and will ask me, at a party, how they can lose more. I am astonished since some of them are thinner than me. Some even come for consultation on weight loss even though their BMI and fat percentage are absolutely in the normal range. So, what prompts this behaviour? I have been studying this pattern in my Delhi patients for the last five years. There are various reasons why this happens. I am going to outline and identify them with some examples.

1. 'When I got married, my weight was less but now my weight has increased by 5 kg.' When did she get married? Fifteen years ago.
2. 'I want to look like that film star.'
3. 'I want to fit into my clothes from eight years ago.'
4. 'I will look better if I lose a few pounds.'
5. 'Everyone I meet is thinner than me.'
6. 'I have this paunch which would go if I lost 3 kg.'
7. 'I have eaten a lot on the trip so now I want to shed that off.'
8. 'I am going to the beach so I want to look super hot.'
9. 'I like to see this number on my scale. I don't care how I look.'
10. 'I have a wedding/party coming up.'

Very rarely will a person understand that each body has a set point of weight; going above that point is easier than going below. At this set weight point, everything in the body is in sync and in harmony. I call this a *nirvana point*. Many people, including me, have tried to play with it but have eventually and invariably landed in trouble. By trouble, I mean that it is too much hard work to go below a certain weight. It's not healthy for the mind, body or the soul.

6. Doing it the *desi* way

Being born and brought up in a typical Indian family, our parents believe that our staple Indian diet is the most delicious. Our hearts and stomachs always have room for a wee bit more, even after a full-fledged meal. No matter how many street food items we keep munching all through the day, nothing can be compared to coming home to savour delicacies cooked by our mothers. On the flip side, we tend to put on those extra kilos with constant indulgence in these traditional diets like aloo parantha topped with tons of butter, or butter chicken with garlic naan, or our very own favourite aloo tikkis. There is just no denying the fact that we, as Indians, are foodies—we eat food, talk food and we definitely dream food. With a plethora of dishes available to tempt our palate, I admit, it does become difficult at times to control those cravings. It may seem impossible for some at first, but you can shed those extra kilos by switching to healthier home-cooked food items. The calorie content in mouth-watering traditional foods can be reduced by cooking them conscientiously, using appropriate ingredients and appliances. The traditional foods are bountiful sources of nutrients. If we take a close look at the constituents of these traditional diets, they comprise of a variety of whole grains, lentils, greens, seasonal vegetables, fruits, nuts and dairy products. A harsh fact and a reality check is that conventional meals have been imbalanced due to consumption of fast foods, ready-to-eat foods and high alcohol intake, teamed with a sedentary lifestyle. The loophole here, unfortunately, is rapid mechanization and urbanization. This lays the foundation stone for non-communicable diseases, popularly known as NCDs. It starts with obesity and goes on to cardiac ailments. Reduction of fats, sugar, refined carbohydrates and alcohol intake, along with increased physical activity, is very crucial at this point of time.

So, the bottom line is that when we don't burn as many calories as we eat, our body is paving the way for an unhealthy and low quality of life. Cooking smartly is the wisest thing to do. Eating food groups the desi way but in a balanced proportion cleaves the way towards a positive outlook and good health.

Chapter 6

Towards a Healthy Lifestyle

Now that we have discussed the various aspects of food and diet in immersive detail, we must look at the big picture that will help us live a happier, healthier life.

1. Behaviour modification

Many diseases and mental illnesses are the result of altered behaviour. Sometimes we are aware of them and sometimes not. Sometimes, we seek help and sometimes we don't. I wrote this book so that all the extra counselling I do for my patients, in limited time, could reach more people.

i. Stress management

I have explained before that stress can lead to bad health. Managing stress is also very important, and the easiest way to do that is to remove the stressors. Stress is so often self-created. It is important to have trust in the higher being. Whatever is happening is for a good cause and the universe is on your side, so you must stop stressing and start living. Respect your body; it is a temple you were born with. The body is the most religious place for us. Don't treat your stomach as garbage. You don't have to eat everything at once because of your reluctance to have leftovers. Keep it for another time. Serve yourself only a small portion to start with. You can even consider donating the leftover food.

ii. Portion control

What is the correct portion? Serving sizes vary with age and your current body condition. If you work out, you need more calories. If you are sedentary, you really don't need more than an amount that will keep your body fit and energetic. Most people misunderstand portions. If you are told to have a serving of fruit, for example, it means a cup of fruit is one serving.

iii. Insomnia or insufficient sleep

Apart from the many adverse effects of lack of sleep, much research has now shown that sleeping less will lead to cravings throughout the day and in turn lead to weight gain. Less sleep is equal to low energy. In such a situation, to increase energy, one eats food—especially simple carbohydrates like sweets/sugars in any other form. If you continue this, weight gain can be as much as 2 lbs/0.9 kg per week.

Sleeping for a minimum of seven hours is a must. Shut off the TV, gadgets and phones thirty minutes before you intend to sleep. Smoking or alcohol can also disturb the sleep cycle, so you must try to minimize these.

Listen to calm music before sleep as it really helps. A friend of mine taught me how to listen to meditation music on my smartphone and to adjust the timer before sleeping.

The regular use of B-complex vitamins, magnesium, herbs and spices like coriander, lemongrass, saffron and L-theanine (a calming amino acid which can be found in green tea) can be very helpful. Chamomile tea, L-tryptophan and 5htp also aid in sleep induction.

iv. Hydration and dehydration

You will never miss water till the wells run dry!

Are you a victim of the 4 p.m. hunger attack? Dehydration is one of the biggest reasons for this. It is amazing that water can lower/curb hunger. Our bodies do not really realize the difference between hunger and dehydration. When we are hungry without a reason after meals, a lot of times it is because of lack of enough water intake. You can try it. After having a glass of water, your hunger might seem to vanish. But if you are still hungry, then it is best to feed yourself rather than think of food.

Case study of a patient who frequently binged

Bingeing on food happens when you consume too much food or too many calories mindlessly. Binge eating is a psychological issue. There may be many people who suffer from it. In general, bingeing on food is abnormal, especially if you are not that hungry.

I happened to have an encounter with this special patient whose story may sound familiar.

A very pretty woman in her 40s came to see me. She already had a diagnosis of depression and anxiety due to which she was on medication under a psychiatrist.

The reason for quoting this example is that many people are depressed, but they don't seek medical help. Once they do, the antidepressants can lead to weight gain and the weight loss journey can become very challenging.

This lady was on medication for a very long time. She had gained a tremendous amount of weight over the last few years and she came for help. She had a sedentary lifestyle and could not exercise as it worsened her palpitations.

She had sleep issues and her psychiatrist was nice enough to discuss her case with me over the phone. We really wanted to help her out with our combined efforts. She had been very upset about her weight gain but there were times she would get really hungry even after a meal and would end up eating chocolate or something sweet.

Her statistics looked like this on her first visit.

Age: 42

Sex: F

Weight: 69.4 kg

BMI: 29.8

Max weight till date: 84 kg

Min weight in last five years: Cannot recall

Previous medical issues: Depression and anxiety

Exercise status: Rare

Diet recall:

Breakfast: Toast and tea

Lunch: Two egg whites, then chicken

Evening snacks: Diet savoury namkeen

Dinner: Two vegetables and roti

Late night snacks: Chips/biscuits/bread/fruit juice from a tetra pack

Social history: Drinks alcohol once in a while and smokes four to six cigarettes per day

Sleep: 6-7 hours

Water intake: Not much

Supplements: Calcium and Vitamin D

Medications: Psych medications

Her lab test results came back; she had borderline high fasting insulin and very low Vitamin B12. If I had checked for the levels of other vitamins, I am sure they would also have come back low.

Supplements were started along with a medication for the insulin resistance. I also asked her to exercise just a little bit at the beginning of the plan.

Her sleeping pattern was different from other people. She would get up late, so there wasn't time for breakfast. She started the day directly with brunch. She was one of the few people whose gluten I stopped completely. I prescribed whey protein for her to have the moment she woke up. She was given proteins, vegetables, jowar roti, nuts and seeds for the rest of the day. She was still struggling with late night bingeing and was on a class of drugs which made weight loss really tough. But neither of us gave up. I was working towards a plan which would reduce her fat percentage but late night sweets were going against it.

I added lots of herbs to her diet as they can really elevate the mood. I also added a calming tea, like chamomile, after dinner.

Something that really comes in handy is passion flower extract, which works as a relaxing agent. She was already on medication for relaxation but sometimes I like to try alternative herbal options as well. I added magnesium supplements for the night and decreased her caffeine intake as she was a patient with severe palpitations.

I prescribed fish for dinner four days a week. Salmon is a very happy food. She loved it and both parties were happy.

She had been struggling with personal issues as well. I didn't dig into them much, but she had a great psychiatrist taking care of her issues. Finally, at the end of two months, she had lost 5 kg. However, this didn't last. She hadn't lost weight at all when she came on her next visit. I had to now strategize differently. She just wouldn't exercise and this made the weight loss plan harder and challenging.

Now I started her on low calorie and normal calorie days. This struck me as the best plan for her as she could have normal calorie days when she was not in a good space mentally and revert to the low calorie days when she was feeling better. This worked to everyone's advantage. Her goals were not realistic—she wanted to drop to a very low number on the scale. But slowly we were working towards that. She had come to me with a lot of doubt and she hadn't been successful even after trying other plans in the past. But she started regaining her confidence and the results began appearing on the scale.

Case study of a thin patient with PCOD/PCOS

I had an interesting encounter with a young girl who was thin. She was very active and a talkative 24-year-old girl. She was really upset over gaining a few pounds. After hearing her concerns, I went into details and checked her body type and realized that she could lose some fat on her abdomen.

Age: 24

Sex: F

Weight: 56 kg

BMI: 24

Max weight till date: 67 kg

Min weight in last five years: 55 kg

Medical illnesses: PCOD/PCOS, mild acne, history of weight gain

Exercise status: Nil

Diet recall: Non-vegetarian

Skips breakfast, has cold coffee with milk

A big lunch consisting of rotis, vegetables, dals and rice

A fruit or cold coffee again as an evening snack, with or without a snack bar

Dinner would be chicken and vegetables

Sleep: 6-7 hours

Plan: On examining her lifestyle and her history of on and off weight gain, I noticed bloating, gas, constipation and sugar cravings—which were all signs pointing to a bad gut. She had visited some famous nutritionists. I realized she needed help in changing her lifestyle; she had gained a bit of weight in the last year and she was not very physically active.

With such patients, I first work on an exclusion diet. Anything that might have been causing her symptoms was removed and then added back carefully. I began by removing all natural or artificial sugar, breads, cakes and pizza from her diet. Pizzas contain yeast which may cause bloating. Milk was removed and I added plain Greek style yoghurt. For a few days, even fruits were taken away.

She needed to rebuild a healthy gut. She was prescribed good probiotics and given less raw food at night. Most people have a fruit before sleeping; it's a habit that will land anyone with a gassy stomach.

I started her on alkaline and vegetarian foods, and then added back eggs and chicken while still keeping bread or yeasty foods away. I also prescribed her to have coconut oil in the morning on an empty stomach. She was given Vitamin B and D supplements to avoid any deficiency. I have to work meticulously on the calorie intake and nutrients in the diet to make sure I don't induce starvation in patients who want to lose weight when they are already at a stable ideal weight. For her, coconut oil would provide energy, act as an anti-fungal agent and an appetite suppressant, and boost the immune system, as she had been having colds and coughs frequently.

Her symptoms disappeared. Her weight remained constant while she started to lose inches and feel a bit more energetic.

She pressed hard for a fad diet for herself but I kept counselling her against it.

Finally, on her fourth visit, we started talking about a health maintenance plan. As on her previous visits, she would come and request a two day detox or some other magical diet because she had a party/wedding to go to.

So, we sat down and discussed the dos and don'ts, and what to do if she ended up eating too many calories at a party. She was given an outline as to how to eat her macronutrients and micronutrients. She didn't need a diet plan to figure that out. She was taught how to manage her evenings out and her alcohol intake, and was given an exercise plan that would last a lifetime. Sadly, she could never have milk again as she realized that she was indeed lactose intolerant. Now that she knew, she could live with that.

She understood her insulin resistance and now avoids processed foods and eats regular well-balanced healthy meals.

2. Socializing

Socializing is a big part of Indian culture. We have a lot

of festivals and weddings, not to mention birthdays and anniversaries. If you are watching your weight, then it's very important to make sure that you are mindful of what is to come. It is okay to go out and be with friends and family but it should not only be about food. When we are out socializing, we are exposed to foods of condensed calories and drinks which are even higher in calories. It is okay to let go sometimes, but one must be careful.

What are the tricks of handling a busy social calendar? The easiest thing is to make sure that you always eat a little bit before you leave the house. The second is to make sure that you compensate for the excessive food or drinks a day before or the next day, and make sure that one of these meals is lean proteins only. Another way to handle this is through exercise. If you are somebody who exercises, just increase your workout. If you are someone who is sedentary—just work out!

When you're at a party or an event, remember to fill up your tummy with healthy food like salads, vegetables and proteins, if available. Keep starch to a minimum (and make sure that you eat less starch on non-party days as well). If your social life is very demanding, then you may want to go for something called intermittent fasting. However, you will have to consult a healthcare provider or doctor to determine if such fasting is suitable for you. Stay away from people who force you to eat or drink extra calories. Make sure you don't overdo sugary drinks like fruit juices and sodas. Stay well hydrated during the party or event. Make sure you sleep well during these periods; otherwise you will lack energy and may end up eating more.

Cheat sheet for a social day

You wake up at 8 in the morning and you know that there is a function in the evening. This is what you do. For breakfast, eat a high protein and high fibre meal—for example, eggs and oat bran. For lunch, go for salads with a liberal extra virgin olive oil dressing and a soup. Some herbal teas in between, and before you leave, have two tablespoons of psyllium husk, add a piece of protein—and then you can go and party. Make sure you don't eat late at night. The next day, have a gap of fourteen hours (including the sleeping period) before your first meal of the day.

> **Case study of a patient who has weight issues due to excessive socializing**
>
> It is difficult to pick out one particular patient from a number of similar patients. I decided to pick one who is under the social pressure of partying but is also a wife, mother and a working woman. She is one of the bravest people I have ever met. She is very dedicated to her work and home, yet in the evening, she lets her hair down and goes to events with her husband.
>
> In her case, there were two specific problems. She had so much stress and lack of sleep that she had been unable to lose weight for years. I thought she was beautiful just the way she was but I also think that due to peer pressure, she had constant anxiety about losing weight. Her life also involved a lot of travel. All these factors meant that this was a very challenging case for me. No medical illness, no bloating,

no issues with bowel movements; she ate little and was quite healthy as per her diet recall. So now, where do you think the problem was?

Stress and lack of sleep were the two biggest issues in her case. She was so pleasant but sad; I would sit for long periods with her in my clinic and let her talk about her feelings. During the conversations, I realized that she was eating very little and not even having happy foods as a part of her diet. She did some form of exercise like swimming daily and made sure she completed 10,000 steps on the pedometer—which alone can make anyone slightly stressed out, especially if you have hypothyroid and haven't been getting enough sleep. Her main focus was just to lose weight in order to look better.

Age: 43

Sex: F

Weight: 73.6 kg

BMI: 42.4

Max weight till date: 95 kg after pregnancy

Min weight in last five years: 65 kg

Previous medical issues: Hypothyroid

Exercise status: Swims daily, goes to the gym sometimes

Diet recall: Non-vegetarian, wakes up at 5 a.m., has tea with milk and no sugar, then methi water, tulsi leaves, two cloves of garlic

Skips breakfast

Brunch: Salad and fruit

Lunch: At home after work, eats whatever is cooked

Evening snacks: Chiwda (puffed white rice that is almost nothing but empty calories, and is non-satiating) or some cookies

Dinner: Mainly proteins

Social history: Alcohol and smoking

Sleep: 7 hours

Water intake: Not a big fan of drinking water

Supplements: None

Medications: None

Plan: First of all, I needed to boost her happiness with happy foods. Breakfast had to be big in her case, but she was skipping it entirely. She was working and she needed the fuel to begin her mornings with a bang. Two whole eggs with coconut oil was how we started, alternating with yoghurt parfait on some days. Lunch had to be leafy green salads with tomatoes and dressing, with extra virgin olive oil and some chopped walnuts and a protein of choice—since she came back home for lunch after a long gap. Evening was the time for some high fibre amaranth cookies and buckwheat cookies with coffee, not tea. Also, before she headed out for exercise, she had to rest well.

Dinner was tricky, as most nights she needed to step out. Therefore, the trick was to eat before leaving. She was given a compulsory homemade vegetable soup along with a dash of ghee and some steamed fish. If she was still hungry, she could have four tablespoons of red quinoa. I let her decide that.

Then came the toughest part of her diet—alcohol and late night eating.

Social drinking is a very personal choice. She could avoid it on some days while on some other days, she had to have two or three drinks. The problem of sleep still persisted as she slept only for three to four hours, which did not help at all in weight loss. There are many studies showing a direct correlation between lack of sleep and weight gain (refer to my chapter on sleep hygiene).

After a few hits and misses, she began to realize that if she was not getting enough sleep, she needed to at least avoid drinking alcohol. It was here that we won. She was given a very strict low calorie diet under strict supervision. I would allow a day in the week for cheat meals as this boosts leptin, which is one of the key hormones in weight control—and also so that she didn't feel deprived of food. She lost 2.5 kg in the first week and her inch loss was even better. Every day was a challenge for her as she needed frequent management. Now I wish to see her every week as such patients need diligent following up in person and constant support over the phone. Their will power is not as strong as some of my other patients and so, as her doctor, I have to do some hand-holding.

3. Tackling addictions: Food, alcohol and smoking

i. **Alcohol addiction** is very common, especially in the suburbs, and there are unfortunately not many AA (Alcoholics Anonymous) counselling centres easily available to the general population in India. However, there are many centres where de-addiction is done and for very little charge.

Family support is a very important part. A person's family should blindly support him/her if he/she has such a problem, or the problem will just increase. I have seen many patients who told me that they drink a lot but hide it from their family. I believe that they drink more because they have to hide it. There should not be a strict rule in the house about alcohol consumption; we should let adults decide for themselves. It is widely known that alcohol is bad for health. So, adults who have a problem know that, and it is for them to decide to get rid of that habit. The family should be supportive in this journey.

Drinking more alcohol increases the risk of such dangers as alcoholism, high blood pressure, obesity, stroke, breast cancer, suicide and accidents. Also, it's not possible to predict who alcoholism could become a problem for. Given these and other risks, the American Heart Association cautions people *not* to start drinking if they do not already drink alcohol. Consult your doctor on the benefits and risks of consuming alcohol in moderation.

Alcohol consumption will eventually lead to weight gain and is detrimental for health—by which I mean that it's a toxin which can be avoided. Our bodies are designed to burn easy fuel first, and alcohol is that easy fuel. The focus of fat or carbohydrate metabolism moves to alcohol metabolism, which results in slowing down of fat burning and increased weight gain, unless you are extremely active and exercise daily.

Also, alcohol is empty calories and has no nutritive value. My recommendation is to avoid it, but if you cannot, here is a better way to deal with it.

1. The big question—something I'm often asked—is how much is okay.

   If you check the American Heart Association website, you will see this: If you drink alcohol, do so in moderation. 'This means an average of one to two drinks per day for men and one drink per day for women. (A drink is one 12 oz. beer, 4 oz. of wine, 1.5 oz. of 80-proof spirits, or 1 oz. of 100-proof spirits.)' Sticking to just one or two drinks might not be possible, however, as it is not easy once you start drinking.

   What is heavy or high-risk drinking?

   Heavy or high-risk drinking is the consumption of more than three drinks on any given day or more than seven per week for women, and more than four drinks on any day or more than fourteen per week for men.

   What is binge drinking?

   Binge drinking is the consumption of four or more drinks for women and five or more drinks for men within two hours.

   This can lead to inflammation in the pancreas, liver cirrhosis and many other medical issues.

2. Try to limit it to weekends (find something better to do when the craving kicks in, like go for a jog or call a friend or go watch a movie).

3. Try to have melatonin; start at 3 mg at night for a short while after talking to a doctor, if curbing the alcohol intake makes you lose sleep.
4. Avoid sweet alcoholic drinks which include tonic water as they have higher calories and affect body weight even more adversely. Some better choices are vodka with water and lime/club soda or caffeine-free diet coke, a glass of red wine (though too much can be fattening), or bourbon and single malt.
5. Space out your drinks, keep hydrating in between and just go slow.
6. Always eat early if you plan to drink at night.

Approximate calories in common drinks

Red wine (175 ml glass)	120
White wine (175 ml glass)	116
Champagne (175 ml glass)	133
Gin and tonic (single)	120
Vodka soda (single)	76
Bacardi white (single 25 ml)	58
Beer (1 pint)	200
Whiskey lemonade (single)	80

You could even use a drink calorie calculator: https://www.drinkaware.co.uk/understand-your-drinking/unit-calculator

ii. Tobacco addiction: In the USA, smoking is banned in most public places. Fines are imposed if someone is seen smoking in public. We, as a country, are still far behind in tackling this addiction. Media advertisements about the risk of cancer are very common. Even a tax has been imposed and increased. A lot of programmes exist to facilitate a person to quit smoking, but they may not be well advertised. I recently heard a radio advert about a nicotine gum which I think is a great government initiative. However, there are way too many people and not enough programmes for such addictions.

I have a lot of doctor friends who are pulmonologists and who are running programmes to help people quit smoking/tobacco-chewing.

To combat nicotine addiction, tobacco users have to agree to quit. On an average, it takes five to six attempts for a smoker to completely quit smoking. So they have to be willing to make the attempt. Some people are in denial, which is not going to help. It may well be a game of will power for some as they go 'cold turkey', which means stopping suddenly and never smoking again. If one person smokes in the family, please don't expect someone else from the same family to give it up. There is stimulation right there.

For some, smoking is associated with habits like drinking alcohol, going out, using the washroom, eating etc. So, these habits have to be dissociated from smoking in order to quit.

Getting away from a certain environment helps.

There are medications that allow you to smoke for some time and give you a smooth transition from smoking to no smoking. For that, you must visit a specialist.

iii. Food and sugar addiction: Food was only a means for survival for the caveman in prehistoric times. Now it has become a part of every event in life. We eat more than we need to. Food was raw in ancient times; tastes like salt, sugar, spices have now become a part of life. Tastes have also altered over the decades.

There was a time when eating simple food at meal times was sufficient, but now we eat in between meals and after meals and before meals.

The most unnatural additives are used in food and make it even more addictive.

Excess sugar consumption causes the body to get hungrier and attract more sugar.

The reason why eating ice cream makes you want more of it is because it triggers insulin release, which tries to bring your sugar down. In normal people, insulin usually goes down subsequently but in pre-diabetics, PCOD patients or diabetics, it remains high, making you hungrier either at that very moment or sometime soon after.

Sugar intake lights up the same areas of the brain as cocaine intake does—a marker of just how addictive and harmful it is.

Our body does not need table sugar, as it is highly processed. There are so many natural sources of sugar in our environment. We must explore them and also teach our kids to choose them over processed sugar.

Natural sources of sugar include fruits, dates, figs, apricots, prunes, sugarcane, palmyra sugar and pure organic honey. The Internet can teach you how to tell the difference between pure and impure honey. Bees can be fed on sugar syrup, which might mar the benefits of honey.

Consuming natural sugar is better than artificial sugar. However, one thing must be kept in mind—overconsumption of these foods will also raise blood sugar, just like using extra virgin olive oil in excess will have the same effect as any other fat. Natural sugars are not addictive per se, but if you put them in everything, insulin will rise, causing fat storage as I explained earlier.

I see a lot of parents struggling to get their child to be fit. We expose our children to different kinds of treats and then try to get rid of the habits that we implanted in them ourselves. It is a sad fact that sugar addiction in children is frighteningly on the rise. If you give your child a well-balanced meal, whether they like it or not, you win the battle against sugar addiction. So many kids don't eat fruits and go looking for cakes and cookies to satisfy their taste buds. So, we must give them more fruits and vegetables.

In my experience, whenever I try to stop a patient's sugar consumption, I get frantic phone calls from them complaining about headaches. It is only natural. The body is trying to detox and that may cause headaches. Just like an alcoholic will face withdrawal symptoms if alcohol is not given to them (alcohol withdrawal is treated with medications), sugar withdrawal is the same—except that it's not so bad and hydration alone will ease it out. However, stopping sugar is a decision one must make. Sugar-free is no solution and we have to get over the taste slowly. Sugar substitutes are chemicals; their overconsumption can result in inflammation of the body and in turn, all the signs of inflammation: aches and pains, bad mood, weight gain and bad skin. The *Stevia Rabaudiana* plant is a sweet herbal substitute that can be used. It won't ferment in the body like other sugars and substitutes. Using too much can even taste bitter.

I suggest that you start a no sugar day once a week and even make it a house rule. It's a good starting point. You will be surprised to see how easily you can give up sugar.

4. Functional fitness

Fitness is a lifestyle, not a temporary gym membership.
By functional fitness, I mean doing minimal exercise to maintain good health. I would like to narrate my own experience. I live in a huge modern society of more than one hundred families. Do you know how many people use the gym? Five people. How many go for walks? Probably ten and that too, mostly a gossipy leisurely walk. The gym is free here but I still don't see many people making use of it. Gyms are about people motivating each other— otherwise, we could just exercise at home. A treadmill at home is seldom used; it is either full of drying clothes or just accumulating dust. **So it is never about the money, but always about priorities**. If your health is not your number one priority, then the medical bills later in life are going to be very troublesome. Always keep in mind that when you get sick, the lives of everyone in the family come to a standstill. I have had that experience too and strongly feel that we must take care of our health so we can take care of our whole family.

Any exercise should cover three areas: strength, cardiovascular fitness and flexibility. You can do these suggested exercises to cover these areas.

Strength: Building muscular strength by using body weight or machines with weights or free weights such as dumbbells.

Cardiovascular fitness: Any activity which increases your heart rate. For example, aerobics, running, cycling, brisk walking.

Flexibility: Stretching, yoga.

Here are the magical things exercise can do for you:

a. Act as an antidepressant
b. Facilitate weight loss
c. Act as an appetite suppressant
d. Increase insulin sensitivity
e. Induce restful sleep
f. Help in hormone balance

The majority of patients I evaluate in my OPD are not engaged in any physical activity as a part of their lives. It doesn't amaze me at all. In fact, I was the same during a temporary phase of my life. People come up with all kinds of explanations for not exercising.

'I don't have time' is the biggest one.

'I work from 7 a.m. to 8 p.m.'

'I have too much on my plate—kids, work, home.'

'I cannot exercise, just give me a diet,' and no explanation why.

'I can't exercise much because I have to then get my hair blow-dried.'

I find these excuses ridiculous, but to be fair, I have made them too. I have bought expensive exercise clothes and equipment and joined gyms only to not do anything at all.

I think many people are scared of the word *exercise*. Exercise doesn't mean going to a gym or visiting a trainer or running a marathon. It means some physical activity which you will be able to stick to for a long time. Joining a gym for three months and killing your body is not the right way.

The American Heart Association published certain guidelines for physical activity: one hundred and fifty minutes a week or 12,000 steps a day could count towards exercise.

So when you start exercising, you must have your doctor's nod on what you should undertake as a fitness regime.

Practically speaking, if you just go for a walk for an hour daily—sixty minutes divided over the day—it will be enough for you. A divided workout is as good as a continuous workout. Out of twenty-four hours, which is a total of 1,440 minutes, how can we say that we don't even have sixty minutes for physical activity when, on an average, we spend 400-500 minutes just eating and drinking and 720 minutes sleeping?

The term 'functional fitness' here refers to workouts or exercises that you can easily incorporate in your life.

Let us start with just seven minutes. For people who have never exercised, this is a good starting point.

So, for starters, just speed walk for seven minutes.

Then you can do pranayama for seven minutes, two or three yoga poses for seven minutes, climb stairs for seven minutes. Basically, you can do any exercise for that much time. However, you must use these seven minutes judiciously to give your body a nudge. Then, when you start feeling good, you will yourself push it to ten minutes, then fifteen minutes, and so on.

A friend of mine inspired me recently when she taught me a few yoga poses. So, every Wednesday for me is a yoga day.

I believe that variety is the key for those who find fitness boring.

So here is your starter schedule:

Monday	Walk for seven minutes
Tuesday	Sit ups for seven minutes
Wednesday	Yoga for seven minutes
Thursday	Climb stairs for seven minutes
Friday	Dance to your song for seven minutes
Saturday	Cycle for seven minutes
Sunday	Mall/window shopping for as long as you want...

Then, you gradually keep putting minutes into the schedule. Challenge yourself.

Other ways to achieve functional fitness include playing with your child. If you don't have children, then form a group and go for walks, join a bicycle group, or play a sport. You don't have the time to go to the gym but still want excellent muscles? Pick up a one litre bottle and do bicep curls just like you would do with dumbbells. In the office, get a stretch band, available on every online shopping website. You can follow the manual that comes with it and start using it at work. You can even do dips on the chair, leg raises while being seated or uthak-baithak (sit-ups, but on your chair).

Surya Namaskar (sun salutation) is the world's oldest form of exercise, and when done repeatedly, it can provide amazing results. Spot running and skipping an imaginary rope for a hundred counts are also very good starts.

I once met the CEO of a corporate giant for weight management and told him that I would like to assess his workplace too. He had this huge office with space unused. I told him that he could get a treadmill in his office and when he is not very busy, he could utilize the time to get on it and just walk. He was very reluctant; he felt shy about how his co-workers might react. What if he sweats? For sweating, I told him to keep the air-conditioning on, and use wet wipes to clean the sweat. I showed him another perspective regarding his co-workers—that the junior staff might get so motivated that they may have even more respect for him. We may feel shy about what people might think, but please keep in mind that it is not their battle—it is yours and yours only.

Finally, the man, who was then pre-diabetic, took my advice seriously. By that I mean that he never got a treadmill to office, but now has an exercise band in and goes for a walk around the office campus during breaks. So, he completes his one hundred and fifty minute target per week.

If you don't understand the math and the explanations, just stick to this basic mantra—walk, walk and walk. A superstar once told me when talking about his fitness regime that when he is not doing his extensive gym workout, he walks an hour daily and even asks his friends and family to just walk for an hour, however they can fit it into their daily routine.

There are other ways that functional fitness can be incorporated into your routine:

- Don't take the lift.
- Walk to the subway/metro.
- Use your car less and walk to the local grocery stores.
- Get up every twenty minutes if you are at a desk as a part of your job.
- Give the cleaning lady an off once in a while and vacuum or broom and mop your home yourself.
- Shovel your own snow.
- Gardening is a great therapeutic/energy-consuming hobby, if you can develop this habit.
- Give your kids a massage often, they love it and they sleep really well.
- Window cleaning can also burn a lot of calories.
- Walk and talk when you are on the phone for a long time
- Fitty kitty: where all kitty members decide to go on long walks on a weekly basis.
- Walk your dog every day; it helps you bond with your pet as well.

To me, these are some of the easiest ways to get rid of **500 calories** without too much thinking. You may not like all of them, so you can pick the one that suits your lifestyle.

I always ask my clients to never take a complete detour away from their natural selves. Only then will we be able to stick to our fitness regimes.

I have listed the ways you can choose to do it.

1. A five minute activity at any time of the day, done several times a day. These activities can include skipping, jumping jacks, pushups, jump squats, etc. If you end up doing twenty minutes in total, you would lose about 250 calories!

2. Replace one meal with a protein shake (at least 20 gm protein in a scoop, with only 0–3 gm carbs, and no more than 10 per cent calories from fat).

   How to make a healthy shake if you do not want to have a commercial readymade one:

   Take a scoop of the powder you bought, pour some unsweetened soy milk, add splenda/stevia if you want it sweet, add lots of ice, blend and drink.

   If you cannot decide on which meal, lunch would be the best option according to me.

3. Cut out one piece of bread/chapati/extra cup of rice and add one glass of water instead to your meal. Cut out the entire carb in the form of starch (for instance, chapati/bread/rice/pasta/noodles/kidney beans) at night, but still eat your vegetables.

4. Spend one hour at the gym doing circuit training with added jogging.

5. Add green chillies to your diet as they contain capsaicin, which will boost your metabolism.

6. Cut out any sugary drinks like Coke or Pepsi or juice from your diet and replace them with sugar free drinks, if you must.

7. Post-partum moms can lose 500 calories a day by breastfeeding.

8. Cut out cakes, chocolates, nuts, cookies, ice creams, pizza and alcohol when you are in the active weight loss mode, as all of them have at least 250-300 calories in one serving.

    You can add them back once you are in the maintenance diet.

9. Cut out your snacking on sweet biscuits/namkeen/ roasted peanuts/cashews/pakoras and replace it with vegetables/salads without dressing/egg whites/fish/any grilled or tandoori meat. At tea time, you can have two marie biscuits only.

10. Cut down on TV, limiting it to two hours a day, and take up any sport/dance/aerobics/yoga as a recreational activity. If this includes your children and family, it is sure to be even more enjoyable and doable.

Case study of a young obese sedentary man

Two years ago, I was visited by a 24-year-old morbidly obese man (morbid obesity is when your BMI is above 35).

He had always been chubby as per his mother. He approached me as I had just moved from America, and they lived close by. He had been to a few doctors and dietitians but couldn't follow any plans as such. Someone also suggested that he undergo gastric bypass. He came to me looking desperate for help. He was a calm young man, very soft-spoken and always smiling. For me, that's half the battle won.

Age: 24

Sex: M

Weight: 125 kg

BMI: 38.6

Max weight till date: 125 kg

Min weight in last five years: 92 kg

Medical illnesses: None

Exercise status: Nil

Diet recall: Non-vegetarian. He eats bread and eggs for breakfast, and rice, chapati, dal and vegetable at lunch. Snacks in the evening are some form of junk food as he feels really hungry at that time. Dinner is mostly curried chicken and chapati.

Sleep: 6-7 hours

Water intake: Forgets to drink water

Supplements: None

Medications: None

I ordered a battery of tests for him and the tests came back in a couple of days. He was absolutely healthy and the blood tests were clear. It was hard to believe, but the fact was that he was obese without any parameters being skewed. One might say that he could go on like this but when he ages, he will either get insulin resistance, or degenerative joint disease, or fatty liver due to excess weight.

The main challenge was that this man left for work at 8 in the morning and was back by 7 p.m. He was wasting a lot of time travelling to and from work and had no time for exercise. However, we had to figure out a time for at least some physical activity.

The challenge didn't end there; he had no time for breakfast, so he always skipped it and by noon, he would eat anything that came his way. I had to fix that before we treaded further.

Since he had a travel time of over forty-five minutes, I suggested a plan on the go. He was driving and so he couldn't eat, but he could drink. Bingo! I knew exactly what to do for him. I gave him a protein smoothie in the morning with fruits and nuts all blended together. He would remain full till 1:30 p.m. and not feel as hungry as he previously did.

Lunch was packed by his lovely mother under my supervision and he was to carry a compulsory salad to work (he never ate salads before this). I started with a plain cucumber and tomato salad, one box of plain homemade yoghurt, one box of vegetables, and some rotis. He had to be full because he had complained that by 5 in the evening, he felt very hungry again. His lunch was full of junk food and junk makes you hungrier than a well-balanced meal. Also, most people are so dehydrated by this time that the thirst can be misinterpreted as hunger. I had to give him a wholesome snack since he was used to eating samosas and bread pakoras or whole packets of cookies for snacks.

For starters, I gave him a well-researched protein

bar that was high in protein and fibre and had no sugar, with two glasses of water or some green tea—whichever he preferred. I had to get his body hydrated. In air-conditioning, most people get dehydrated and don't even realize it. Once he came back home, his mother would make him another balanced meal with less starch and more vegetables—maybe a soup without corn flour along with a decent serving of protein. As far as exercise was concerned, I asked him to walk for thirty minutes post dinner. His challenge was to eat his meals slowly. He, like most other patients of mine, would gobble up the food or eat in front of the television. I asked him to sit calmly and enjoy the food slowly. I asked him to practise mindful eating. Late at night, he would be on the Internet or watch TV but would get hunger pangs. When he started eating slowly, he was no longer hungry at night. He was also asked to sleep earlier than midnight to avoid unnecessary eating. He didn't need a midnight snack as he wasn't diabetic and therefore his dinner would be sufficient for him. As time went by, he lost 26 kg in sixteen weeks, roughly averaging 1.6 kg a week. Along with his diet, I also prescribed a good multivitamin, Omega 3, and a protein supplement for his mornings. He never felt any lack of energy and he gave up junk food. He did attend a few parties where there was alcohol and outside food but he would be careful not to go over his daily budget. It was a huge learning experience for him.

Now, he goes to the gym three times a week, has increased calorie intake due to heavy weight training and comes in once in a while to check with me if he is doing everything right. He has changed his lifestyle; he eats a full breakfast and doesn't rely on smoothies only. He manages his meals as well. He eats all the important food groups—even vegetables, which he wasn't fond of at the beginning of the programme. The last time he was at my clinic, he weighed 96 kg—a total loss of 29 kg in eight months. This was learning at its best, and he is a good role model for people who have a lot of weight to lose but no patience or hard work to do so.

5. Sports as a hobby

Sports don't necessarily have to be played for competition. They can be a great hobby that maintains your health on a long-term basis. You don't have to choose a sport which is tiring. In fact, it should be chosen as per your age and convenience. Don't choose a sport for which you have to travel a long distance from your place or one that requires too much equipment. These reasons might make you discontinue it as a hobby for a long time. For example, if you are a 60-year-old man and you want to pursue football, it may not be the greatest hobby. You must instead opt for something like golf. Similarly, a woman over forty who has never been a sportsperson and wants to engage in some form of sports as a hobby should pick either a zumba class or some form of aerobic dancing, yoga, swimming, salsa etc.

Most parents don't play any sports even as a hobby, due to which the kids don't cultivate this habit for themselves either. Even if you are not a very active person, you can begin some form of light sport at any time in your life. When you are active yourself, you set an example for your child. This kind of bond can be extended during holidays and weekends as well. For example, if you like kayaking, you can take your kids along for the same sport. If you like biking, you can take your kids for biking treks, which are quite common these days. While holidaying, most people end up spending too much money and time on food. I would rather suggest that you spend more time on sporting hobbies, and for that you have to be in a good physical shape. There are a lot of indoor games that can be taken up as a hobby; for example, chess, ludo and carrom. But remember, these will not help you expend any energy, as they are sedentary games. The easiest physical activity as a sport and hobby, for anyone, is walking. Walking is the single most effective sport, which can be done anywhere, anytime and at any pace. Another point I would like to mention is that when parents or families go out for picnics, we usually mainly concentrate on food. We should, instead, plan the picnic around a sporting activity—either visiting a bowling alley or going to a park for badminton, volleyball or just passing the ball around (dodgeball). Some popular hobbies are listed below so you can pick one of your choice and convenience. Some of these are high impact sports activities while some are low impact.

High impact: Swimming, bicycling, running, hiking, skiing, badminton, tennis, water scooter, skipping, powerlifting.

Medium impact: Horse riding, canoeing, kayaking, archery, hopscotch, rowing.

Low impact: Frisbee, fishing, etc.

As we age, most of us become more sedentary than before, which leads to weight gain—especially around the abdomen. We wonder if it's our metabolism that has become slower. In truth, it is the decrease in our level of activity that leads to a pot belly. So if you don't play sports as a hobby, it's more likely that weight gain will be inevitable. Therefore, I suggest that a sporting hobby should be inculcated from a very young age so that you remain healthy and your bones remain stronger in the long term.

It is not advisable to start a high impact hobby later in life. If you're someone who used to have a sporting hobby (or played sports) and you gave up, then I suggest that you get back to your old hobby slowly, as your muscle memory will recognize it and soon you will be back at your game. If you have developed a disability and you cannot play sports as a hobby, you should still not give up. I am sure you'll find another interesting sports activity to pursue. As I know, a lot of people who love sports can't give up, so they start alternate forms of sports which suit their body type. For example, if a marathon runner can't run anymore, he or she can at least swim or do static bicycling at home, or even rowing, which can be an excellent indoor sporting hobby as well. The indoor rowing machine is a much underused sporting device and should be used more often.

Discover your interest by yourself when it comes to being active or playing a sport, because each person differs from the other and you have to love what you do. You don't need to have the same interests as your friend or relative. Your friend may like taekwondo and you may like tai chi. It is completely up to a person as to what makes them the happiest.

6. Yoga and weight loss

Yoga is the most relaxed form of exercise and it calms you down. In fact, it is not just a form of exercise. It is a lifestyle. It is a union of the ego and the self with the divine self and spirit. Most people mistakenly think of yoga as a religious practice or just reduce it to different 'postures' which can be quite difficult to master. Yoga is an ancient Indian science which is a holistic approach towards life. It means that your spirit, mind and body are in union with one another. When a person starts pursuing yoga, it is not about the asanas. It is about the energy flow in the body and the breathing (pranayama) techniques. The first rule of yoga is to practice good breathing. Yoga for weight loss means that you have relaxed your mind and cleansed your spirit. Only then do you pursue the physical asanas to achieve flexibility, strength and fat loss. Yoga is not just a form of exercise practised by saints, which is a common misconception. Yoga is no longer limited to India or the Asian subcontinent. It has become a worldwide phenomenon.

So let me briefly discuss how to use yoga for weight loss.

1. Make sure that you practice breathing. Exhale and inhale in full capacity with your mind empty of all thoughts at the same time. This is the first step. As you know, stress can cause weight gain, so to

begin practicing yoga for weight loss, you need to de-stress. If you can do even three to five minutes of calm breathing and practice this three to four times a day, you will be able to de-stress and de-clutter most of your thoughts.

2. Practice meditation, whether it is guided or not. Meditation does not mean listening to music and being quiet. Meditation means that you clear your mind of all thoughts, no matter what they are. It's a state of mind which is very hard to achieve. Meditation can be done by guiding yourself, taking guidance from a friend or teacher or even from guided meditation videos that are available online, with variable durations. You can pick any of the videos as per your time and convenience. There are also apps available on Google Play and Apple Store which can show you how to meditate.

3. There are various yoga poses for weight loss. I am not a yoga expert at all, so I had to take advice from friends and people who do yoga and know which asanas can lead to more weight loss. There are different forms of yoga—namely, power yoga, ashtang yoga, vinayasa yoga, hatha yoga, iyengar yoga, kundalini yoga, sivananda yoga, and many more subtypes in different parts of the world. Vinayasa yoga is almost like a dance form where movement and breath are synced and music is usually used along the way. Ashtang yoga is similar to vinayasa but usually performed in a sequence of asanas, without music. Iyengar yoga was founded by

B.K. Iyengar, a famous yogi from India. It's slower in pace, has very specific postures and uses breath control through pranayama. Power yoga is high impact hatha yoga often accompanied with music and has a lot of core and upper body exercises. Sivananda yoga uses the five basic principles— breathing, relaxation, dieting, exercise and positive thinking. Kundalini yoga is the activation of energy centres in the body. It is like exercising with spiritual enlightenment, where self-awareness is the key.

When you start yoga for weight loss, go slow because most of the time, if the asanas are not done properly under the guidance of a teacher, people end up having injuries. I would suggest going for easy poses rather than trying to do difficult poses in the beginning. Once you practice the easy poses, your body will become more supple and flexible enough to try out difficult poses. When you start doing yoga, you must also remember to accompany it with a good diet of fresh foods and limit your consumption of alcohol, cigarettes and processed foods. As I said earlier, yoga is a lifestyle. Anything that causes stress like junk food, alcohol, smoking or drugs can negate the benefits of yoga as a weight loss tool.

A lot of people think that going to the gym or running marathons is the only way to lose weight, but if yoga is done the right way, focusing on the mind, body and spirit, the benefits can be phenomenal. I have personally seen many people on plant-based diets and yoga who have achieved tremendous amounts of weight loss and feel extremely active, and are doing well in life. However, the last word is to have the right teacher and the right guidance before you start this form of practice.

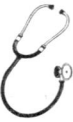

Chapter 6

Medications and Medical Advice

1. Understanding the need for prescriptions and avoiding taking medicines on your own

I didn't learn about food as medicine at medical school. There, I only learnt how to diagnose an illness and treat it with the best possible medication. Is it wrong to say that food can be used as medicine? Most of the ancient science of Ayurveda is based on that.

Pharmaceutical companies are flourishing by making new drugs and drug combinations. Every day, I see a new pharmaceutical company rising and every single one of them is surviving because diseases today have increased manifold, which means that there is business for everyone.

Why is that? The prevalence of diabetes, heart disease, rise in cholesterol and high blood pressure has become more common than tuberculosis. There was a point in time when India and other developing countries were struggling with new treatment strategies for diseases like malaria or tuberculosis, but now, you will find that lifestyle diseases have taken a lead. Everyone has either a friend or a family member who is diabetic or has high blood pressure. India has the second highest number of people suffering from diabetes, obesity and now metabolic diseases in the world. The reasons are simple—**overeating, sugar, processed foods and lack of exercise.** Pre-diabetes among kids has gone up, and it is frightening how many will grow up to have diabetes. Is this not an economic burden?

Our healthcare industry is trying to set up prevention clinics. Efforts are in place to set up clinics for diabetes and high blood pressure diagnosis. But while the government is trying to take steps, most people are ignoring the many adverse effects of such diseases. Every day, leading newspapers are reporting how our country is seeing a rise in diabetes and obesity. However, are we changing the sugar intake in schools? Here is my experience. I started advising against adding sugar to milk and the response I got was that kids would not drink it. We must collectively try to change that attitude. Kids don't know what to eat but we, as parents and educators, have to teach them just like we teach them math and science.

I happened to go to a school in Rajasthan and saw kids getting fried snacks daily during their break. I also observed that most kids had very high BMI. You could have a skinny child and yet they can have diabetes, as they can accumulate fat internally by eating junk food. Junk food not only affects your body, it also has a serious effect on brain development. Parents and teachers must look at the quality of food consumed by the students in school.

Going back to medications for these chronic illnesses: often, when I prescribe medication, I am asked about the side effects. Yes, they are not free of side effects, but the biggest side effects come from the food you eat. That toxic metabolic load of food every day in your diet is changing your gene structure, causing inflammation and leading to obesity.

Most patients still prefer medication over exercise. Medication is highly over-prescribed. I often hear, 'I would rather pop a pill than walk in the park.' NO. That's not how it works. Exercise, water and food are free medicines. Yet the rich pharmaceutical industry will push for medications first. People need to realize this sooner rather than later. We take medications from our friends in developed nations and have ignored our science of Ayurveda which says, 'Food is Medicine'.

I can clearly recall so many occasions when I discontinued a medication and introduced new foods, and the patients resisted that change. But those who adapt change their lives forever.

Self-medication and its dangers

It is a sad truth that, in our country, most prescriptions are over-the-counter. So often people just ask the chemist for a medication, bypassing a doctor visit. Self-medication is rampant and its side effects are even worse.

Regulatory bodies are trying to regulate this easy availability of drugs. Over-the-counter availability of medication was probably meant to make them easily available. You can get them from a chemist once in a while, but only when you land in serious health trouble.

Sometimes, most chemists are not even pharmacology graduates. They really don't have any idea about drug salts. Would you go to a restaurant and eat food made by a waiter? We need a chef. It's as simple as that. We must let specialists do their job. When I came back from the USA, all I was using were the generic names of medications. Whenever I wrote a generic name on the prescription, I would get calls from the patients that the chemist does not recognize it. That is just so disheartening. But now there is a new government rule of using generic names only. This will definitely improve our system.

I see so many patients who take medication because it benefitted their friend. Now that is a very serious issue. You haven't seen a doctor, yet you popped a pill. The end result is that you will visit the emergency room sometime soon to get your system fixed. Sometimes, the harm can be irreparable.

When it comes to medical advice, most people also refuse to take their medication. If a patient is highly diabetic and needs medication, then no lifestyle change can cure them. However, taking medication alongside making lifestyle changes is the way to go sometimes.

It is a myth that once you start taking tablets, you become addicted and can never come off them. ALL MEDICATION IS NOT ADDICTIVE.

The truth is that once you start the medication and make certain lifestyle changes such as cutting back on sugar and junk food and incorporating exercise in your routine, the dosage will go down, and eventually, you will be able to discontinue the medication. I have had patients who have stopped medication for diabetes and hypertension after starting on a healthy plan. Dieting is not a word in my dictionary. There has to be a permanent change in your life with a few deviations once in a while.

Can we reverse the damage to our body by changing our life at any point in time?

Yes, it is like when you give up smoking and instant benefits are seen in your lung capacity. If you control what you eat, most diseases will be kept at bay. After all, as the old adage goes, 'We are what we eat.' However, just as food can be used as preventive medicine, some medications are very necessary for life. Supplements and medication for any illness should be treated seriously.

Some people give up medicines in favour of herbal supplements. That is not a smart choice. I am not very sure about what herbs you can or cannot take, but I am quite sure that if you do not take your essential medication, you are going to get very sick—which might even lead to you ending up in a hospital. I have encountered so many patients taking something called 'bhasam' (ashes) and substituting it for medication. Most of these things contain heavy metals and therefore, you must be careful. Screening for heavy metals in these cases is very important as these can lead to kidney/liver/brain injuries. These herbal solutions are most misused for weight loss and diabetes. You have to accept that you cannot get rid of these if you do not change your lifestyle.

I have also seen people abusing pain medications. There are several medicines for pain that are banned in the USA, but still continue to be used here. I don't want to get into the legalities, but having frequent pain medication without consulting a doctor can land you in a lot of trouble. Pain medication abuse is very common; it directly affects the kidneys and can even cause kidney failure. A good friend of mine is a nephrologist and the number of patients she sees in a day is unbelievable. Medication induced nephropathy is a very common diagnosis.

These cases mainly come from the suburbs, which means that over-the-counter medication and the lack of doctor visits are the primary causes. These people don't have disposable income to spend on treatment or dialysis and it is easy to become helpless in such situations.

I just hope that a lot of people can read this and seek proper help. This is my primary objective in writing this book, the inception of which was three years ago. However, it is only now that I feel that I am equipped to write an effective book after having seen so many cases in my clinic.

I will emphasize here again. Please don't be a doctor for yourself or for others if you have not studied medicine. Let the right people take care of you, your family and friends.

2. Fat-loss surgery

Many patients ask me if they can get a gastric bypass surgery (a weight reduction gastric surgery), and some even ask about liposuction. Most of these people are looking for shortcuts to weight loss, though some actually require these surgeries for therapeutic reasons. Most people forget that behaviour and lifestyle modification is the most important aspect of weight loss, whether you get a surgery or not.

i. Bariatric surgery

If, however, you are having bariatric surgery, you should give yourself two to three months to prepare. This is because post-surgery, your appetite will go down, while the greed remains. The patient might start feeling upset about not being able to eat enough and, therefore, some mental preparation has to be made by the patient or the patient's family before they think about gastric bypass surgery.

Then there is the important question: who qualifies and who doesn't?

There are some set protocols by the ASMBS (American Society of Metabolic and Bariatric Surgery) that qualify or disqualify a person for surgery. A BMI of more than 35 with comorbidity of diabetes and obesity, or a BMI between 30 to 35 with uncontrolled diabetes (especially in the presence of major cardiovascular disease risk factors) is required. If you have a BMI above 35 and you are at risk due to heart disease, diabetes, sleep apnea, high blood pressure or osteoporosis, you could be a candidate for bariatric surgery.

Pros:

There are many pros of this surgery—a high rate of cure

for diabetes, weight reduction, reduction in risk factors for heart disease, better activity levels, better mental performance and decreased metabolic disease risk. There can also be an improvement in blood pressure.

Cons:

Sometimes, you might lose too much weight. Or, at times, the weight might all come back. There can be malabsorption and vitamin deficiencies. There can also be alternate addiction to alcohol or other addictive substances in some cases. Since gastric bypass is a major surgery, other significant risks like infections and blood clots cannot be ruled out—or even gall stones and kidney stones.

Care after bariatric surgery:

Initially, you must visit your MD/MB every month, then after every three months, then six months and then yearly. Make sure you see a doctor who is aware of the side effects of bariatric surgery and is able to help you if the symptoms of dumping syndrome or hypoglycaemia appear. Make sure you work with a professional who can advise you on a good food diet that speeds the healing process and is able to correct vitamin deficiencies in a timely manner.

ii. Liposuction

Liposuction was designed to take out fat from the stubborn areas of the body. The ideal candidate is someone whose BMI is normal but who has fat deposits in areas that are not responding to diet and exercise. The technology has improved a lot since the first liposuction. Now, more and more areas can be liposuctioned. However, one must remember that after liposuction, there is a certain kind of healthy lifestyle that one needs to lead because one can very easily regain the weight in that area if one is not careful. As in bariatric surgery, even before liposuction, one must prepare mentally about changing their lifestyle, making sure to include exercise in the daily routine. One has to also ensure that they are active and not eating junk food too frequently. Liposuction will remove fat only from subcutaneous areas which are directly under the skin, but not the fat around the organs, which is called visceral fat. Visceral fat is the most dangerous form of fat and is responsible for fatty liver and heart disease. So, if you are thinking of getting liposuction, you must keep that in mind. With bariatrics, visceral fat will be targeted because the fat will be removed from all over the body, whether it is subcutaneous or visceral.

Pros:

Removal of fat in a stubborn area can give you more confidence and help you look a certain way.

Cons:

Infection, scarring (which should not be an issue with the latest technology due to small gauge needles), not a lot of weight loss as fat is lighter than muscle and there is a risk of regaining fat in the same areas if not followed with a healthy lifestyle.

3. Using your kitchen as your medicine cabinet

a. Fruits

i. Tomato

- **Source of antioxidants**
  Tomatoes are a source of antioxidants like Vitamin C, Vitamin E along with beta–carotene. They lower the risk of developing cataracts, strokes and cancer.
- **Contains protective substances**
  Quercetins, a flavonoid found in tomatoes, along with lycopene, have many protective effects on the body.
- **Improves vision**
  Lycopene present in tomatoes improves vision health along with preventing night blindness.
- **Improves heart health**
  Beta carotene and lycopene present in tomatoes are antioxidants and therefore, reduce the oxidative damage to the heart, prevent formation of clots and also help in maintaining the cholesterol levels.
- **May prevent enlarged prostate**
  Lycopene may be responsible for blocking the production of hormone responsible for the growth of the prostate gland. Being an antioxidant, tomatoes control the growth and the onset of cancer of the prostate.

ii. Banana

- **Source of potassium**
  It is a good source of potassium, which helps in regulating blood pressure.

- **Increases the energetic activity**
  Starch present in less ripe bananas boosts energy for a long period. Sugar present in very ripe bananas, eaten after exercise when the muscles are exhausted, can improve stamina.
- **Improves the bowel health**
  Starch present in less ripe bananas leads to better bowel movement, thereby easing constipation, whereas very ripe bananas are used for treating diarrhoea.
- **Induces sleep**
  Bananas have carbohydrate with little protein, which stimulates serotonin, responsible for uplifting mood and inducing sleep.
- **Contains iron**
  Iron is present in a high amount in bananas which helps in treating anaemia. Bananas also contain copper, which produces red blood cells thus not only preventing anaemia but also improving blood circulation in the body.

iii. Apple

- **Reduces the blood cholesterol**
  Soluble fibre and pectin found in apples may help reduce blood cholesterol levels. It may also help reduce low density lipoprotein.
- **Prevents constipation**
  The fibre and fruit acid combination in apples helps in preventing and treating constipation. Also, the antiviral properties in apple help in treating diarrhoea.

- **Reduces arthritis and gout**
  Apples help to treat joint pains as they are responsible for ejecting unwanted substances from the body. This is because of the combination of fruit acids and antioxidants in apples.
- **Fights illness**
  The pulp, skin and juice of apples all have substances that destroy viruses and have anti-cancer properties.

iv. Pineapple

- **Strengthens the immune system**
  Pineapple is rich in bromelain, which helps the body fight against viruses which affect it.
- **Helpful in breakdown of proteins**
  Pineapple contains enzymes which help in the breakdown of proteins and improve digestion.
- **Reduces blood clotting**
  Pineapple enzymes may reduce blood clots which in turn, reduce the risk of getting a heart attack or stroke and also improve the digestion process.
- **Helps in strengthening of gums**
  Pineapple contains astringent which helps gums from the attack of harmful bacteria.

v. Orange

- **Protection against cancer**
  It contains phytochemicals which help in fighting against cancers of the skin, lung, breast and stomach.
- **Helps in lowering cholesterol**
  Oranges are rich in soluble fibre 'pectin' which helps in

the lowering of blood cholesterol.

- **Protection against diseases**
  Oranges are rich in Vitamin C, which neutralizes the free radicals and protects us from diseases.
- **Good for skin**
  Oranges are rich in beta carotene which provides protection to the skin against free radicals and also reduces signs of ageing.

vi. Lemon

- **Helps in treating indigestion**
  Lemon juice helps in treating indigestion and constipation problems. It also acts as a blood purifier and cleansing agent.
- **Helps as an immunity booster**
  Lemon contains Vitamin C and antioxidant properties which help in boosting immunity and fighting certain diseases.
- **Absorption of iron**
  Eating Vitamin C rich foods helps in the absorption of iron in the body and in treating anaemia.
- **Helps in boosting brain system**
  Lemon also contains potassium which helps in the proper functioning of the brain and reduces brain fog.

b. Vegetables

i. Spinach

- **Rich in iron**
  Oxalates present in spinach are a source of iron. Iron

is needed for energy alongside being a component of haemoglobin, which carries oxygen to all parts of the body.

- **Regulates blood pressure**
  Potassium present in spinach maintains the blood pressure levels.

- **Rich source of folate**
  Spinach is a rich source of folate which reduces the risk of babies having spina bifida.

- **May prevent age-related macular degeneration**
  Irreversible blindness is due to the age-related macular degeneration which can be prevented by eating spinach, a rich source of carotene.

- **Rich source of antioxidants**
  Spinach, being rich in antioxidants like carotene and Vitamins C and E, reduces the risk of developing heart disease, stroke, cataracts and cancer.

- **May lower the risk of cancer**
  People who eat more leafy vegetables are at a lower risk of developing any kind of cancer.

ii. Fennel (Saunf)

- **Improves digestion**
  Fennel reduces flatulence, bloating and belching. Also, fennel oil is added to gripe water for children.

- **Antispasmodic**
  Fennel seeds can ease colon and intestinal cramp pains.

- **Acts like oestrogen**
  Due to the oestrogenic effect, fennel consumption has been used for a long time, for e.g., to increase the

production of breast milk and to stimulate menstruation.

- **Reduces wheezing**
  Fennel oil syrup helps to clear cough.
- **High in potassium**
  Fennel helps in managing blood pressure levels.
- **Reduces constipation**
  Fennel seed powder is used as a laxative. It stimulates the gastric juices and bile production and, therefore, helps in proper excretion.

iii. Coriander

- **May help improve skin conditions**
  Antifungal and antioxidant properties of coriander are important for clearing skin disorders like dryness, fungal infection and eczema.
- **May help heal mouth ulcer**
  The oil present in coriander known as citronella has antimicrobial properties which prevent ulcers in the mouth from getting worse. It also prevents bad breath.
- **Anti-allergic properties**
  The oil present in coriander reduces the effects of allergies and rhinitis. The oil also reduces allergies caused due to insects, plants, food and other agents.
- **May help regulate blood sugar levels**
  Coriander also helps in the absorption of sugar and in regulating blood sugar levels. It helps patients in lowering the risk of an insulin spike.

iv. Tulsi

- **Prevents heart disease**
  Vitamin C and antioxidants like eugenol present in tulsi prevent heart diseases. Also, eugenol helps in reducing the cholesterol levels in blood.
- **Powerful antioxidant, also reduces stress**
  Antioxidants and Vitamin C present in tulsi reduce the damage done by free radicals. They also manage the blood pressure levels and reduce stress and inflammation.
- **Oral disinfectant**
  Tulsi is known to be an oral disinfectant; it destroys most of the microorganisms in the mouth. It also prevents the growth of oral cancer caused due to tobacco.
- **Improves dental health**
  Tulsi has many astringent properties which prevent teeth from falling out by making the gum hold the teeth tighter. It also kills the bacteria that can cause dental cavities, bad breath and plaque.

  Tulsi has shown many psychological and physiological effects as well.

v. Cabbage

- **May help in the treatment of peptic ulcers**
  A study was published many years ago that cabbage juice is an effective home remedy which helps in treating peptic ulcers.
- **Improves digestion and gut health**
  Fermented cabbage is good for improving digestion and gut health.

- **A rich source of folate**
  Raw cabbage is a good source of folate, which is good for pregnant women.
- **Powerful antioxidant**
  Cabbage is rich in antioxidants, which lower the risk of cancer, heart disease and stroke.

vi. Cucumber

- **May help reduce the risk of cancer**
  Cucumber contains phytochemicals which have anti-cancerous properties and also boost the immune system by eliminating free radicals from the body.
- **Helps in reducing cholesterol**
  Sterols present in cucumber help in lowering bad cholesterol in the body.
- **Good for heart health**
  Cucumber is a good source of potassium, which lowers blood pressure and also reduces the chances of getting stroke and CVD.
- **Reduces ageing effects**
  Cucumbers are widely used in skincare products as they protect the skin from ageing effects.

vii. Carrots

- **Prevention against lung cancer**
  The beta carotene present in carrots reduces the chances of getting lung cancer and also other forms of cancer.
- **Lowers blood cholesterol levels**
  Raw carrots help in lowering blood cholesterol levels.

- **Improves eyesight**
  Carrots are a good source of Vitamin A which helps improve eyesight.
- **Good for heart health**
  Carrots are a good source of beta carotene and eating a raw carrot every day reduces the chances of getting a stroke.

viii. Chilli

- **Reduces blood clots**
  Chillies help in lowering the risk of a heart attack or stroke by improving circulation and reducing blood clots.
- **Helps in reducing cough and cold**
  Capsaicin found in chillies stimulates secretions, which helps in clearing mucus and reduces congestion.
- **Improves digestion**
  Chillies increase gastric acid secretion in the stomach, which enables digestion and also helps in destroying bacteria present in food.
- **Helps in weight loss**
  Capsaicin may stimulate cellular organisms and alter lipid catabolism and thermogenesis, which helps against obesity.

ix. Mint

- **Helps in treating dizziness, headaches**
  Mint has anti-inflammatory properties which help in treating headaches and dizziness.
- **Helps in improving dental health**

Mint leaves have antiseptic properties that treat gum infection. Chewing mint leaves helps in alleviating toothaches.

- **Promotes eye health**
  Mint contains Vitamin A which helps in maintaining good eye health. Deficiency of Vitamin A can lead to night blindness or other eye disorders.
- **Helps in weight loss**
  Mint stimulates the body to digest fat. It quickly absorbs food nutrients and converts them into energy.
- **Helps in digestion**
  Mint soothes irritable bowels and gastric ulcers. Mint is fibrous in nature and can help in preventing constipation.

x. Curry leaves

- **Rich in antioxidants**
  Curry leaves contain antioxidants and anti-bacterial, anti-inflammatory properties which help in elimination of bad bacteria from the body.
- **May help in treating constipation**
  The fibrous nature of curry leaves supports bowel movement, which helps in getting relief from constipation.
- **Protects liver from stress or damage**
  Curry leaves protect the liver from oxidative stress and harmful toxins. The anti-oxidative properties of curry leaves help in stimulating the organ to work properly.
- **Prevention of skin infection**
  It contains anti-bacterial, anti-fungal properties as well

as antioxidant properties which help in skin infections like acne, and fungal infections.

xi. Onion

- **Helps in strengthening immunity**
  Onions are the natural way to strengthen immunity, as they contain Vitamin C and phytonutrients which are believed to build up immunity.
- **Prevention against cancer**
  Onions contain phytonutrients like quercetin that help in fighting free radicals and can help prevent cancer.
- **Helps in detoxification**
  Onions contain sulphur compounds and amino acids which help in clearing toxic substances from the body.
- **Helps in digestion**
  They are rich in fibre, which acts as a laxative and helps in bowel movement and promotes digestion.

xii. Garlic

- **Reduces the risk of heart disease**
  Consuming garlic helps in reducing the risk of cardiovascular disease as it contains antioxidant properties. It also regulates blood pressure as well as blood sugar levels.
- **Cancer prevention**
  Studies shows that the consumption of garlic on a daily basis helps in colorectal cancer, and helps ease stomach discomfort.
- **Enhances the immune system**
  Garlic boosts immunity because of the presence of

certain compounds. It also helps in fighting microbes or bacteria.

- **Can help in reducing asthma attacks**
Consumption of garlic on a daily basis reduces hypersensitivity and also helps reduce the occurrence of asthma attacks.

c. Spices

i. Cinnamon

- **Rich in antioxidants**
Cinnamon contains antioxidants called polyphenols which help in fighting against free radicals.
- **Prevention against heart disease**
Cinnamon helps in lowering cholesterol and LDL levels and also reduces blood pressure.
- **Prevention against cancer**
Cinnamon is toxic to cancer cells and reduces their growth, eventually leading to their death.
- **Helps in fighting against infections**
Cinnamaldehyde, a component present in cinnamon, helps the body in fighting against infections.

ii. Turmeric

- **Anti-inflammatory**
Turmeric has antioxidant properties which help the body in fighting against infection and, in turn, enhance the immune system.
- **Beneficial for metabolic syndrome and obesity**
Turmeric improves insulin sensitivity, suppresses

adipogenesis and reduces blood pressure and is particularly beneficial when combined with piperine.

- **Reduces joint pain**
  The anti-inflammatory properties of curcumin help in reducing joint pain and inflammation.
- **Improves brain function**
  It helps in the regeneration of neurons and prevents degenerative processes in the brain.

iii. Black pepper

- **May help in digestion**
  Black pepper helps in digestion.
- **Helps in treating cough and cold**
  Black pepper is a natural home remedy for treating cough and cold when combined with honey.

iv. Asafoetida (Heeng)

- **Good for stomach problems**
  It has anti-inflammatory and antioxidant properties that help in problems like indigestion, upset stomach, intestinal gas, flatulence and irritable bowel syndrome (IBS). It is also considered useful in treating food poisoning.
  You may even add a pinch of asafoetida while cooking food.
- **May help relieve menstrual issues**
  It helps get rid of menstrual pain, irregular menstruation and heavy blood flow during menstruation. Asafoetida (heeng) boosts progesterone secretion and promotes smooth blood flow. You can try adding a pinch of asafoetida in buttermilk (chaach) on a daily basis.

- **Prevents cancer**
  It helps protect the body from free radicals. Studies show that its anti-carcinogenic property helps stop the growth of malignant cells and thus prevents cancer.

v. Ajwain

- **Helps in weight loss**
  Ajwain stimulates the appetite, which helps in weight loss. It also has a laxative effect.
- **Improves digestion**
  Ajwain stimulates the gastric juices, which help in better digestion. It also helps during constipation, bloating and cramps.
- **Boosts immune system**
  Essential oils present in ajwain contain antioxidant properties which help in boosting the immune system.
- **Prevention of kidney stones**
  Ajwain helps to prevent the formation of kidney stones.
- **Helps in bronchitis and asthma**
  Taking ajwain in warm water helps in relieving cold. It is also good for bronchitis and asthma.

vi. Cumin

- **Improves digestion**
  Due to its magnesium and sodium content, taking roasted cumin powder helps in relieving constipation problems and improves digestion.
- **Contains iron**
  Cumin contains iron which helps in increasing haemoglobin levels and treats menstrual problems.

- **Helps in fighting premature ageing**
  Cumin contains anti-fungal properties which fight against microbial infections and help in fighting premature ageing, wrinkles, age spots etc.
- **Prevents food-borne illnesses**
  Cumin has anti-viral and anti-bacterial properties which help in fighting infections and food-borne illnesses.
- **Improves bone health**
  Calcium in cumin helps in increasing the bone density, thereby delaying the onset of osteoporosis.

vii. Ginger

- **Helps combat nausea and morning sickness**
  Research has shown that the intake of ginger on a daily basis helps to combat nausea in pregnant women and helps in morning sickness.
- **Helps in digestion and helps relieve flatulence**
  Ginger stimulates bile and promotes digestion, relieving flatulence.
- **Helps in fighting cold and coughs**
  Ginger contains a warming effect on the circulation of blood and also helps in fighting cold and coughs.
- **Acts as an immunity booster**
  Ginger acts as an immunity booster and helps in cleansing the lymphatic system. Ginger prevents the accumulation of toxins in the body.

vii. Triphala

- **A very powerful antioxidant**
  Being the extract of three berries—amalaki, bibhitaki

and haritaki—it is rich in antioxidants.

- **A powerful immune system builder**
  It improves digestion and constipation. It protects your liver, heart and eyes.

- **One of the remedies used in ancient India**
  It has now become globally popular because of its wonderful effects on the human body. Do not use triphala if you are on certain medicines that need to be titrated since triphala can inhibit absorption of these medicines. Make sure you discuss it with your physician before using it.

d. Dairy

i. Yoghurt

- **Protection from harmful bacteria**
  Yoghurt, induced with acidophilus, prevents the occurrence of gastroenteritis and vaginal thrush. It can also prevent peptic ulcer, urinary tract infection and food poisoning.

- **Restores gut health**
  Live yoghurt helps in restoring gut health. The gut health reduces due to the intake of antibiotics which affect the body's ability to fight infection.

- **Improves immune defence**
  Live yoghurt increases the ability of body cells to fight harmful bacteria as well as antiviral infection.

- **Improves diarrhoea**
  Clinical trials done on children and adults show that children eating live yoghurt recovered from diarrhoea

in three days as compared to children on antibiotics. Even adults using antibiotics recovered faster when given yoghurt as well.

- **Improves skin health**
  Zinc present in yoghurt helps in soothing dry, pale skin, along with acne caused due to the exposure to UV rays.
- **Manages cholesterol level**
  Lactobacillus acidophilus present in yoghurt decreases the low density lipoprotein. High LDL may induce a risk of coronary heart disease. Regular intake of yoghurt reduces the risk of heart disease.

e. Nuts

i. Walnut

- **Improves heart health**
  The two essential fatty acids, linoleic acid and alpha-linoleic acid help in reducing blood cholesterol levels. Also, they prevent the formation of blood clots.
- **Acts as an anti-inflammatory agent**
  The essential fatty acids, linoleic and alpha-linoleic acids, reduce the itchy and scaly skin conditions along with rheumatoid arthritis.
- **Rich source of nutrients**
  People with small appetite benefit from the high calorie concentration found in walnuts.
- **Improves brain health**
  The photochemical present in walnut improves brain signalling along with the formation of neurons.

- **May help prevent cancer**
  The Omega 3 fatty acids and antioxidants found in walnut prevent the growth of cancer cells, including breast, prostate and pancreatic cancer.

ii. Flaxseed

- **Regulates blood sugar level**
  Flaxseed is rich in both soluble and insoluble fibre. Fibre regulates the blood sugar levels, especially for patients with Type II diabetes.
- **Improves blood health**
  Flaxseed is rich in manganese which can be used to improve both bone and blood health which also fights problems like anaemia and osteoporosis.
- **Reduces plaque formation**
  Lignans present in flaxseeds reduce plaque development.
- **Acts as an anti-inflammatory agent**
  Lignan, phytochemicals and Omega 3 present in flaxseeds reduce inflammation and promote the recovery of tissues.

f. Grains

i. Oats

- **Helps in lowering blood cholesterol**
  The beta glucan fibre which is present in oats helps in lowering bad cholesterol as well as cholesterol in general.
- **Helps in easing out the problem of constipation**
  Oats are rich in both soluble and insoluble fibre which helps in preventing the problem of constipation.

- **Helps in reducing hypertension**
  Oats help in combating high blood pressure.

g. Herbs

i. Tea

- **Rich in antioxidants**
  The flavonoids present in tea help in slowing down the ageing process. Some studies suggest that it also plays an important role in preventing cancer.
- **Good for heart health**
  Tea is good for reducing blood clots which, in turn, helps lower the risk of heart attack and stroke. It also helps in reducing cholesterol, LDL and triglycerides.
- **Helps in fighting against flu**
  Tea increases the body's immune response against the flu virus.
- **Reduces tooth decay**
  The fluoride content present in tea helps in reducing tooth decay.

Chapter 7

Some Simple Recipes to Try at Home

SOUTH INDIAN STYLE CAULIFLOWER RICE

INGREDIENTS

1 head of cauliflower
2 cloves of grated garlic
5-6 curry leaves
½ tsp mustard seeds
½ tsp olive oil/ghee
Salt as per taste
Black pepper as per taste

METHOD

1. Grate the cauliflower head nicely.
2. Take a pan, add ½ tsp of olive oil and heat it.
3. Add mustard seeds, curry leaves and grated garlic and sauté for a few seconds.
4. Add grated cauliflower, salt and black pepper as per taste.

5. Add boiled rice to this.
6. Cover the pan and cook for five-ten minutes.

Cauliflower rice is ready. You can serve it with curried vegetables like dal and kadhi.

~

ALMOND FLOUR PANCAKE (BADAM KA CHILLA)

INGREDIENTS

4 tbsp almond flour
1 beaten egg
½ tsp baking powder
A pinch of salt
1 tsp vanilla extract
½ cup almond milk/water

METHOD

1. Add all the above ingredients in a bowl and make a batter out of them.
2. Heat a skillet and coat it with ghee. Pour the batter on the skillet.
3. Cook for about two minutes until the sides of the pancake firm up.
4. Flip the pancake to the other side and cook for about two minutes more.
5. When the pancake is ready, for topping you can add blueberries, pure maple syrup or roasted seeds.

~

ALMOND FLOUR BROWNIE

INGREDIENTS

2 tbsp butter, softened
½ cup sugar (erythritol)
1 egg
¼th cup unsweetened almond milk
1 tsp vanilla extract
1 cup almond flour
¼th cup unsweetened cocoa powder
1/8th tsp sea salt
1 tsp baking powder
¼th cup chopped almonds

METHOD

1. Add butter and sugar in a large mixing bowl. Add beaten egg, almond milk and vanilla extract and whisk them all together.
2. In another bowl, whisk together almond flour, cocoa powder, sea salt and baking powder. Add it to the butter mixture and blend just until mixed. Stir in chopped almonds.
3. Coat the baking pan with non-sticking cooking spray. Pour batter into the prepared pan and spread evenly. Bake for thirty to thirty-five minutes.
4. Remove the pan from the oven and allow the brownies to cool slightly before slicing and serving.
5. Garnish with more chopped almonds and enjoy the brownies with a cup of black coffee.

OAT BRAN AND EGG UTTAPAM

INGREDIENTS

4 tbsp oat bran
2 full eggs
½ cup chopped vegetables
Salt as per taste
½ tsp ghee

METHOD

1. Take a bowl, add oat bran, beaten eggs, chopped veggies and salt and mix them well.
2. Heat a skillet, add ghee and pour the batter on a skillet.
3. Cook until the sides of the uttapam firm up, for about two minutes.
4. Flip the uttapam to the other side and cook for about two minutes more.
5. Your oat bran uttapam is ready! Enjoy it with mint chutney or homemade coconut chutney.

~

OAT BRAN AND BESAN CHILLA

INGREDIENTS

2 tbsp oat bran
2 tbsp besan
½ cup chopped methi/palak
Salt as per taste

Pinch of chilli powder
Pinch of ajwain
½ tsp ghee

METHOD

1. Mix oat bran, besan, methi, salt, chili powder and ajwain in a bowl.
2. Add water (according to the thickness you want) and make a batter.
3. Heat a skillet, add ghee and heat it for a few seconds.
4. Pour some batter on the skillet and heat it for one minute.
5. Flip the chilla from the other side and heat it for one minute more.
6. Enjoy your oat bran and besan cheela with mint chutney or curd.

~

COCONUT MILK/ALMOND MILK

INGREDIENTS

1 cup almonds/grated coconut (fresh/dry)
1 cup water

METHOD

1. Blend almonds/coconut properly with water.
2. Strain the mixture with coconut/almond in a glass.
3. Your coconut/almond milk is ready. It can even be used for making pancakes or cold coffee.

BESAN AND GOND LADDOO

INGREDIENTS

2 cups besan
1 cup organic ghee
A handful of chopped nuts
1 cup erythritol
1 cup gond (boswelia resin)

METHOD

1. Deep fry the gond crystals (boswelia resin) in ghee on medium heat for a few seconds, crush them and keep them aside.
2. Roast besan flour in the remaining ghee on medium heat till it is brown.
3. Add erythritol, chopped almonds and gond to the roasted besan and roll them into balls.
4. Your besan and gond laddoos are ready! You can eat them as dessert.

~

CAULIFLOWER ROTI

INGREDIENTS

½ kg cauliflower florets
5-6 tbsp psyllium husk
2 full eggs
½ tsp salt

Almond flour or coconut flour for dusting and aiding the rolling process

METHOD

1. Add the cauliflower florets to a blender jar, blend them properly into a powder form.
2. Add psyllium husk, eggs and salt until the ingredients are well mixed. Let the mixture stand for about five-ten minutes to allow the psyllium husk to bind the ingredients. Turn out the dough on a plate or work surface.
3. Use coconut flour to dust the rolling pin. At first, pat the dough ball down into a larger round shape and roll out the roti.
4. Roast these on a non-stick frying pan or a griddle pan on the stove top. Cook on low heat and when the underside is cooked, flip over and cook the other side.
5. Serve cauliflower roti with vegetables and chutney. You can even make rolls with the stuffing of dry vegetables.

~

OATS POHA

INGREDIENTS

½ tsp mustard seeds (sarson)
4 tbsp rolled oats
7-8 curry leaves
½ tsp turmeric powder
Salt as per taste

1 chopped green chilli

1 tbsp lemon juice

2 tbsp chopped fresh coriander

½ cup water

½ tsp oil

METHOD

1. Take a non-stick pan and add oil on it, heat it for a few seconds on a medium flame.
2. Now add mustard seeds and curry leaves and heat for thirty seconds.
3. Add chopped vegetables like peas, carrot, broccoli, bell peppers and cook for two minutes.
4. Add turmeric, salt, red chilli powder and lemon juice.
5. Now add oats and ½ cup water. Stir well.
6. For garnishing, you can use chopped coriander.

~

YOGHURT AND BLUEBERRY SMOOTHIE

INGREDIENTS

1 cup curd

2 tbsp oats

A handful of blueberries

8 almonds

2 tbsp roasted seed mix

METHOD

1. Take a blender and blend all the ingredients together for one-two minutes.

2. Pour the mixture in a glass and serve.

You can even add ice cubes for a chilled drink.

~

KETO COCOA BALLS

INGREDIENTS

4 tbsp coconut flour
1 tbsp unsweetened cocoa
2 tbsp unsweetened almond butter
1 tsp erythritol

METHOD

1. Mix all the ingredients in a bowl.

2. Roll the mixture into balls to make laddoos. Your keto cocoa balls are ready!

~

CRISPY OAT BRAN AND GARLIC CHICKEN

INGREDIENTS

100 gm of chicken breast
2 or more fresh cloves of garlic
4 tbsp oat bran

METHOD

1. Crush garlic and put it in a bowl with oat bran. Add a touch of sea salt.

2. Add chicken and coat it well with the garlic and oat bran mixture.
3. Put the coated chicken in an air fryer for at least five-ten minutes or lightly fry it on a pan.

~

SNACK OPTIONS (VEGETABLES AND EGG RECIPES)

OATBRAN MUFFINS

INGREDIENTS

2 cups oat bran uncooked
Stevia as per your taste or ¼ cup(s) pure maple syrup
2 tsp baking powder
½ tsp salt
1 cup(s) almond milk/buttermilk
2 egg whites, slightly beaten
2 tbsp vegetable oil
½ cup(s) raisins (optional)
¼ cup(s) chopped walnuts (optional)

METHOD

1. Heat oven to 425°F.
2. Line twelve medium muffin cups with paper baking cups or spray bottoms (only with non-stick cooking spray).
3. Combine the dry ingredients; mix well.
4. Add milk, egg whites, maple syrup and oil to the dry ingredients.

5. Mix just until the dry ingredients are moistened.
6. Add walnuts and raisins, mix until just combined.
7. Fill prepared muffin cups until they are ¾ full.
8. Bake for fifteen to seventeen minutes or until golden-brown.

Baking tip: Add ½ cup fresh or frozen blueberries or ½ cup (1 medium) mashed, ripe banana to the batter.

~

GREEK/HUNG YOGHURT

INGREDIENTS

1 litre of milk
1 tsp of live curd culture

METHOD

1. Boil whole milk and then let it cool to room temperature.
2. Add a spoonful of yoghurt prepared the previous day (should be a live culture. The yoghurt we make at home is 'live', with many bacteria).
3. Set the milk for the night or for six to seven hours at warm temperature.
4. Once the yoghurt is set, hang it by putting in a mesh/ very thin silken cloth over a container that will drain out the excess water.
5. You can let it hang for one hour or more depending on the texture you want.

6. Your greek yoghurt is ready!

You can use the drained water in cooking. Please note that it has about 10-12 gm protein in one cup.

~

ANJEER/DATE BAR

INGREDIENTS

10-12 dates
1 cup of chopped mixed nuts
2-3 tsp of chia seeds

METHOD

1. Chop the dates and figs.
2. Heat a deep pan.
3. Throw in the nuts and mix them together till you get a dough-like consistency.
4. Remove from heat and cut into small-sized bars.

~

HOMEMADE BREAKFAST: HIGH PROTEIN CEREAL

INGREDIENTS

1 cup rolled oats
½ cup chopped nuts (pre-toasted)
2-3 tbsp of maple syrup
1 tbsp pumpkin seeds
1 tsp chia seeds

METHOD

1. Roast the oats in a dry pan till they are brown.
2. Add nuts, seeds and maple syrup and roast for another two-three minutes.
3. Let it cool and store in an airtight container.
4. For best results, serve with almond milk or plain yoghurt (dahi).

Chapter 8

The Cheat Sheet

When you are planning to have a cheat meal, you have to take care of a few things.

Everyone is aware that cravings are real and you cannot avoid them at some point, especially when you are following a particular diet plan or weight loss plan. So, enjoy your favourite food fully and satiate your cravings with good food.

Why are cheat meals okay once in a week?

Many people think that cheat meals are not good and they will end up gaining weight because of them. However, many cases have shown that those who choose to have a cheat meal now and then while following their nutritional plan have been more successful in losing weight. Not having a cheat meal is therefore not a good idea.

Here are some things to keep in mind while considering the pros and cons of having a cheat meal.

1. A cheat meal is advisable for good mental and

physical health. If you are on a calorie-restricted diet for a longer period, your body metabolism will become slow and will eventually plateau. A cheat meal once in a while will help regulate your hormones and also boost metabolism.

2. When you are planning your cheat meal, you must take care that you enjoy the food. While having a cheat meal, you have to take care of the nutrient content. So go for a fat, protein and carb combination and focus on the protein source rather than going for junk foods. Choose nutrients over sugar.

3. Try to avoid your weakness and never go for a cheat meal when you are hungry, otherwise you will end up overeating.

4. Do not forget to burn your extra calories. Regular exercise will help you remain motivated.

5. Unplanned cheat meals are more dangerous. So, if you are going for a cheat meal, plan in advance.

6. Overindulging and frequent cheat meals are, of course, not good for health.

7. Portion your meals carefully and avoid overconsumption. It is a cheat meal, not a cheat day.

Cheat sheet while travelling

Healthy eating while travelling is a real challenge. Fast food is easily available on the go and can be tempting. The best course is to be prepared—carry your own food if possible or carry protein bars and packed foods, which are slightly healthier than buying a fried sugary donut. Healthy crackers can be taken with cheese or hummus, or you can pack roasted snacks in your bag till the time you reach a restaurant and order your vegetables, proteins or salads.

Here are some of the options for snacks you can eat on the road:

- Whole wheat pancakes with fresh fruit
- Fruit/yoghurt smoothies
- Chicken/cheese satay with grilled veggies
- Fresh/dry fruits
- Protein bars
- Lentil salads
- Grilled veggies with paneer/chicken/fish
- Whole grain crackers with dips
- Fish with sweet potato fries
- Baked sweet potatoes
- Baked vegetables
- Dark chocolate
- Whole wheat pasta/spaghetti with veggies
- Black coffee with buckwheat/coconut flour cookies
- Falafel with hummus
- Pizza with meat and veggies
- Fluffy scrambled eggs
- Sweet potato chips with salsa
- Greek yoghurt (plain is best)
- Cottage cheese
- Hard-boiled eggs
- Soups

- Whole-grain pasta salad
- Turkey and cheese sandwich on whole-wheat bread
- Hard-boiled egg and cheese in a whole-wheat pita
- Cucumber and whipped cream cheese on whole-wheat bread
- Peanut butter and jelly on rye
- Grilled chicken, lettuce, tomato and mustard in a whole-grain wrap
- Hummus with sliced tomato, pepper and cucumber in a whole-wheat pita
- Roasted chickpeas
- Graham crackers
- Whole grain cookies
- Fruit snacks
- Whole grain dry cereal
- Coconut water
- Oats porridge
- Loads of water

Simple snack ideas under 100 calories

You must remember that when you jog for ten minutes at average speed, you lose 100 calories—and when you walk for twenty-five minutes, you roughly burn the same amount of calories.

First of all, buy yourself some zip lock bags and a cup measure from a kitchen store.

You can mix and match all of these ideas and make your own packets:

14 almonds (raw, unsalted)

Half cup or 4-5 unsalted walnuts (edible part)

20 baby carrots/1 cut cucumber

50 raisins

1 pear

1 apple

1 cup blueberries

1 full stalk of celery with a hung yoghurt dip

2 tablespoons dry roasted unsalted Bengal gram or chickpeas

½ cup of wheat bran flakes from Kellogg's

1 ounce (fistful) of dry roasted unsalted soy nuts

4 Marie biscuits

1 Laughing Cow low fat cheese cube with 2 crackers

5 pieces of salami (processed food)

1 whole wheat toast (dry)

1 tablespoon pea

Things to be kept in mind while ordering food from outside:

When you order from outside, make sure you include more vegetables and protein. Usually restaurant portions are high, so don't feel shy about sharing or packing the leftovers. Just avoid ordering fried items, and go easy on desserts. Outside food is laden with hidden sugars and salt—always keep that in mind. Healthy options on the menu are easy to find. Sometimes just ordering appetizers can be enough. So order only appetizers and go easy on the main course. Hydrate well before the meals. Salads and dressings should be ordered separately.

Avoiding seasonal weight gain:

These are the five ways to keep your metabolism up this winter.

1. Have one tablespoon of roasted/raw pumpkin seeds twice a day.
2. Have peppers of all colours, especially green. If you cannot have them, get tabasco sauce and add to every meal.
3. Have green tea once or twice a day with no milk or sugar. Lemon or artificial sweetener/cider can be added.
4. Do some high intensity early morning workouts for just ten minutes. You can follow some YouTube videos.
5. Add cinnamon to whatever you can. If possible, add cinnamon bark boiled in hot water, which is more effective than powder. You can even add powder to beverages if you don't have anything else.

Festive cheat sheet:

Come Diwali or Christmas or Halloween, we are exposed to sugary, mouth-watering treats, evoking festive nostalgia from when we were growing up.

Here are some easy steps for the holiday season, when you just cannot get away from all the food.

1. Don't deprive yourself of the sweets you have really been waiting to eat. Eat a piece slowly and

before you go for the next one, drink a big glass of water or a huge cup of green tea. Green tea should be increased to three cups a day at least during the holiday season.

2. Add fifteen extra minutes to your high intensity workout with every extra ounce of sweets. Jump rope a hundred times more if you have to.

3. Try not to eat other carbohydrates and starches if you plan to binge on sweets.

4. Eat more chillies to alter sweet cravings.

5. Proteins decrease sugar cravings, so you must increase their intake significantly.

6. To stay fit, you can have pure protein days when you only eat protein for at least two or three days before or after you plan to sin. Eat unlimited amounts of egg whites/chicken/fish/tofu/greek yoghurt/protein shake with zero carbs. The only carb allowed will be oat bran cereal with milk or water, cooked at home. Ask your nutritionist/ doctor how much is okay for your body.

7. Stay away from wine as it will pack pounds in your middle. If you have to drink alcohol, drink only vodka with club soda and lime.

Kickstart your weight loss regime with this sample plan

Here are some more tips to maintain a diet and workout in your daily routine, especially for working professionals.

Note that you would want to first check with your physician before starting any weight loss programme.

You should not eat under 1200 calories per day, or your BMR (Basal Metabolic Rate) will drop and you will gain the weight right back.

1. Start the day with some spot jogging for five minutes and a few stretches. Try to squeeze in a quick workout. Also have two glasses of water.

2. Eat a full healthy breakfast to keep yourself from starving at other times of the day. A healthy breakfast includes whole-wheat toast/egg white/ fresh fruits/low fat cheese/low fat milk/tea or coffee optional. For roti/idli lovers, just avoid the fried stuff. Coconut chutney is also good.

3. Snack in about three hours. Some good options are an apple or a pear or ten almonds/ten walnuts (loaded with Omega 3 fatty acids). Nuts keep you full and are laden with protein. Sugar-free gum is another good idea.

4. If you can pack your lunch to work, that's great. Just choose from the following options: a sandwich with salad and cheese or firm minced tofu, grilled tandoori chicken, upto two chapatis/rotis with two cups of dal. Avoid potatoes. Add at least one full cup of low fat yoghurt to your meal. Have one glass of water around this time. Eat slowly and enjoy this meal, taking a real break from work.

5. Snack time should be again in three hours. This time, you can have a whey protein shake, plus one or two glasses of water, or a fistful of roasted unsalted channa/soy nuts/low fat cheese.

6. Exercise for about thirty minutes to an hour (get a brisk walk, or cycle, or work out on a treadmill/cross trainer/weights, or golf, or swim).

7. In the evening, your body is preparing to get lazy, so are your intestines. So don't overeat at this time. Make healthy choices for your dinner whether you eat out or at home. It should ideally be $1/3$ protein, $1/3$ carbohydrate and $2/3$ vegetables.

Avoid frequent desserts. You may reserve them for weekends. Avoid fruits at night as they ferment in the colon during the night.

If you drink alcohol and can't stop, then limit it to one drink with lots of ice, and go slow. You can try chamomile tea at night, as it is super relaxing. Some patients have told me that they stopped alcohol/desserts completely after starting to drink this tea before bed.

You must remember that studies have shown that 7-8 hours of sleep keeps your hunger in check during the day.

Epilogue:
Loving Yourself

'You have to love yourself because no amount of love from others is sufficient to fill the yearning that your soul requires from you.'

— Dodinsky

Self-love and self-respect are two of the most important things for a human being. If you don't love yourself, it will be very hard to make anyone happy. Most of us don't understand the meaning of self-love. Buying things for ourselves, getting too materialistic, spending too much or just thinking about ourselves before the needs of others are not examples of self-love. Loving yourself is when you respect your body as well as your mind. Loving your body means you love the way you look and don't put junk in your body or fill it with poison like alcohol or drugs. You treat it with fresh and preservative-free foods. You don't consider your body to be a dustbin, thus clearing the plate on your table instead of just leaving the food on it when you're full. In such scenarios, I always suggest that you fill up only half of the plate at a time so that you don't waste food.

We go to temples to pray and find peace—which is fine—but ultimately the peace and love is within us. Your body is like a temple. If you worship it, you will feel positive and you will find no need for external gratification of any sort. Most people have a wrong or negative image about themselves, which leads to a lot of stress—and to cope with that, people end up finding comfort in food. A negative self-image can be very destructive. Therefore, the first thing you should do every morning is stand in front of a mirror and tell yourself that you are perfect the way you are, and that you will seek help for anything that is wrong with your health. Everything else will fall into place. I have seen patients who are thin and fit but still have a negative self-image and are constantly aspiring to lose more weight and look 'fitter'. We should not let commercial magazine covers or the media let that happen to us; we will only end up aspiring to look like someone else. All of us are unique in our own ways and we must always try to love ourselves. The whole idea of this book is to help you understand your own body, your own diseases, and figure out a plan for yourself—a health plan, a fitness plan and a spiritual plan—so that you are your own first priority. Remember, if you make an effort to love yourself every day, you will see how your perspective towards the world changes. You are your own competition. Be in love with the person you see in the mirror.

Everything is beautiful about you and no one else can love you the way you can. You live with yourself till you die, so you are the only one who can love yourself forever. Keep motivational quotes, frame them, keep them at your workplace and at home and only hang out with people who make you feel positive about yourself. Let go of negative energies. You must walk away from that person or thing that makes you feel low about yourself. Do not compare yourself with anyone. As I said, God made each body composition different, so comparisons are the worst thing that you can do to yourself. In fact, a lot of parents also end up comparing their kids to other kids, which actually leads to low self-esteem in children, who grow up not loving themselves and end up being depressed. This also makes it very difficult for them to fall in love with themselves all over again when they grow up.

Each chapter in this book is a lesson for you, whether it's about food, shopping, sports activities, medication or fitness. How you read it and adapt to it will be entirely up to you. I have tried to touch upon the basic problems a common person faces when it comes to health, and, as I mentioned earlier, this is not a weight loss book. This is a book which you can use to maintain your health, prevent illnesses and, occasionally, for weight loss.

नितिन गडकरी
NITIN GADKARI

मंत्री
जल संसाधन, नदी विकास, गंगा संरक्षण,
सड़क परिवहन, राजमार्ग एवं पोत परिवहन
भारत सरकार
Minister
Water Resources
River Development, Ganga Rejuvenation,
Road Transport, Highways and Shipping
Government of India

Afterword

I love eating street food, especially Mumbai and Marathi style. I am also very passionate about work and put in hours to fulfil my duties, whatever has been assigned to me. These two things really made me gain weight early in life, my metabolism was compromised and I developed diabetes. During my tenure as Party President, I decided to reduce my weight and improve my general health. I opted for bariatric bypass surgery. Post surgery, my weight came down considerably but my diabetes was not really under control.

In 2013 someone mentioned Dr Anjali Hooda Sangwan, who had shifted from USA and was an Obesity, Post-Bariatric Surgery and Advanced Metabolic Specialist. Since then I have been with her as a patient and she advises me on all aspects of lifestyle changes like Medication, Nutrition, Supplements, Food, Snacks and Fitness. Due to time constraint and old habits, I am not able to fully commit to these changes on a few occasions but I try to follow her instructions as much as possible. Her commitment and compassion towards her work is extraordinary and so is her knowledge in her chosen domain.

I wish she continues in her quest of finding patient-centric solutions in Preventive and Integrative Medicine and combines modern medical practices with our Vedic knowledge to heal the body from inside out. This is my belief that prevention is better than cure and this is the future of Medicine. I hope she reaches millions of homes with this book and empowers people with her knowledge.

11th June 2018

Nitin Gadkari

Room No. 210, Shram Shakti Bhawan, New Delhi-110 001
Tel. : WR,RD&GR (011) 23711780, 23714663, 23714200, Fax : (011) 23710804
Tel. : RTH&S (011) 23711252, 23710121
E-mail : minister-mowr@nic.in, nitin.gadkari@nic.in